GW00758709

Special Thanks

My thanks and praise must go to my wife of over
50 years Elizabeth (Lizzy) without whom this book
would never have been written.

It was her idea and determination to catalogue my
memories and then to disseminate them into this book.
She wrote the book using my words and her intellectual
insight and, once started, she was determined to complete it.

Ultimately, however, this story does not belong to me, as
I was just a journeyman through time, and this is reflected
in my recollections.

WITH BEST WISHES
FROM
William & ELIZABETH
02/2021

First paperback edition January 2021

Published by CPI Group
www.cpi-group.co.uk

Book design and editing by Vanessa Marchant-Williams at
www.whitespacedesignco.co.uk

A special thanks to the following for their assistance in proof reading our manuscript, providing content advice, and for generously giving of their time; Dr Mairi Rennie, Mr Jim Malcolm LTC (and for his music), Mr Anthony Froggatt and Mrs Carole Froggatt

ISBN 978-1-8383020-0-9 (paperback)

www.drtyrrellspublishing.co.uk

CONTENTS

THE ABC MINORS' SONG

(The song was sung to the tune- 'Blaze Away')

We are the boys and girls well known as

Minors of the ABC

And every Saturday all line up

To see the films we like, and shout aloud with glee

We like to laugh and have a singsong

Such a happy crowd are we.

We're all pals together.

We're minors of the A-B-C.

**The final line was shouted
at full blast - especially the A-B-C.**

OUR SONG

"There is a mouldy dump

Down Windsor Way

Where we get bread and cheese

Three times a day

Egg and bacon

We don't see

We get sawdust in our tea

We are gradually

Fading away, fading away, fading away!"

THERE IS A MOULDY DUMP

Composer: Andrew Young 1838
arr (1) Leonard P. Breedlove 1850
arr 2) Jim Malcolm 2020

(If sung as a round: unison to bar 20 and
2nd voice to start again from bar 31.)

Processing by Music Seasons, tel. 02392-342300

This music was specially arranged for "Down Windsor Way" by Jim Malcolm LTC.
Reproduced with kind permission of Jim Malcolm LTC.

FOREWORD

This is an historical perspective of our time spent in the care of Barnardo's and seen through the eyes of William the youngest of four brothers. It is not intended to suggest that their experiences in any way reflects life in Barnardo's care in modern times. My book is dedicated to the team at Barnardo's past, present and future, for providing help and support for those in need. The "Tyrrell" boys remain eternally grateful to them.

The Barnardo Family Relationship Team have this to add.
This book offers a rare insight into the lives of four young brothers who, due to circumstances beyond their control, found themselves in the care of Barnardo's for eight years. It has been a pleasure to work closely with William and Elizabeth on this project which clearly is a great labour of love. Although the day to day life that the author describes is historic and does not represent modern Barnardo's care it is, from a sociological perspective, extremely interesting and therefore an important record of childcare in former times.

PREFACE

In the blink of an eye

I have a story to tell that in my opinion, is not only unusual but possibly unique. The circumstances behind the themes and events that are discussed below were probably fairly common in terms of children entangled within a poor parental relationship. The events that occurred during our time in care, however, are almost impossible to replicate.

Today, children finding themselves in a similar situation to ours, are unlikely to be raised using the same care "model" that we experienced. Institutional childcare during the 1940s-1950s most often meant physical separation of children from their parents, as in our situation, into homes that were hundreds of miles away from their usual domicile. In contrast to today's social model of assimilating children-in-care into a "family" style environment we were raised in grand, but nevertheless rather stuffy old houses, in some of the most isolated parts of the UK. Also, rather than being raised by a mother/father key role model, it was made clear to us that our parent figureheads were strictly nurses and matrons. A few of the nurses were rather unkind to us and, at times, appeared to be heavy handed and acerbic. They would think nothing of exerting very severe punishments in order to restore "discipline" into the children. Throwing a "bed wetter" into a bath of cold water or washing a young child's mouth out with carbolic soap if they answered back or were cheeky are good examples of their "care" for us.

Thankfully, as a result of changes in attitudes to child care, it is very unlikely that the anecdotes and experiences that I intend to share with you will ever be replicated again. Our society has changed to such an extent that the scenarios that I am about to present to you would be morally unacceptable today. Times have changed, the world has changed, social views and opinions have changed. Meanwhile my memories have remained fairly constant and true and I feel that now is the time to share them with you while I still have the capacity to recall them.

The following account is intended to demonstrate two important ideas concerning "family" life in post-war working class Britain.

Firstly that the premise behind the start of my journey, as a six month old child, will serve as a cautionary reminder to future generations of parents. Primarily this concerns the decisions that adults make and the subsequent methods that are employed in the execution of their plans of action. There is much at stake and a wrong decision at an early stage may, as we shall see, have lifelong repercussions. I consider that my life story serves as a clear demonstration of just how wrong, or just how right depending upon your point of view, the decision-making process can be.

Secondly it demonstrates, to all, the role of nurture and how it can play a powerful role in influencing what and how that end product, in terms of adulthood, actually turns out. Although there is a consensus of opinion it is often assumed, even taken for granted, that we will grow and develop into well-rounded, well-balanced individuals as a result of the values instilled into us from the stable upbringing, assistance and support from loving and indulgent parents.

That is for an ideal world. For many this model of care sometimes fails. The scenario that follows relates to a situation that confronted my siblings and me when we were only nippers in the late 1940s. It would appear that our future lives were pre-destined not only on the basis of the inadequate decisions that were made by our parents but also by the aftermath of living an institutionalised life for so many years. Although I was only a baby at the time, for some of my older brothers, the consequences of such decision making were to have an overwhelming influence in their later lives. After all before being taken into care they were young children free to play as they wanted. This was brought to an abrupt halt when they were suddenly, rather like the containment of a young wild animal, prevented from doing as they wished. They could only speak when told to and could only eat and sleep when told to. Once in care they found themselves at the bottom of the pecking order, in terms of authority among their peers, and had to struggle to regain any resemblance of the independence they formerly enjoyed. Suddenly any control over the events in their lives was gone and any free will or personal liberty was taken away and no longer under their control.

Welcome to institutional life in the late 1940s.

The circumstances that surrounded the dilemma that we brothers faced, has been shrouded in mystery and falsehoods by our parents. By doing some simple calculations, however, we soon became aware that my mother was "with child" at the time that we were taken away. Unfortunately for Tenby, our name for our father because he lived in a Tenby Road, he wasn't on the scene during that period, or for the previous few months, as he had yet to be demobbed by early 1947.

A young and inadequate couple had been forced into a corner and made to face the reality of their situation. Rash choices were made. It was never made clear to us why the extended family failed to intervene to ensure that we were not separated from them. This has always been a bitter pill to swallow as our mother had two siblings, as did my father, and in fact his sister was a maiden aunt!

According to my mother our father abandoned her to her own devices and, under the extreme personal circumstances she found herself in, there was no alternative but to place her children into care. In time she began to believe this. She also alleged that the "Barnardo people" were instrumental in ripping her youngest child, namely me, from her arms as we were taken away to begin the next chapter of our lives in their care. Now out of her sight it became clear that we were also out of mind and it would be many years before we were reunited. I am pretty sure that the immediate aftermath of this event would undoubtedly have been very traumatising, however I have also come to recognise a certain irony that existed throughout the ensuing period. Thus throughout our years in Barnardo's we became more and more institutionalised and dependent upon them. Furthermore, all our thoughts and decisions were made for us. We were given no opportunity for any form of independence or self-input at all in our everyday life. In contrast to this our parents went on, in their separate lives, to enjoy a full life with their new families.

During the early 1990s we were able to visit the Barnardo Headquarters at Barkingside to review the case-notes of our time spent living in the various homes. It was during this visit that we were made aware of the true circumstances behind the family breakup. It seems that it was our mother who started the ball rolling by abandoning the family home and with it her four sons. According to the records our father was forced to place his youngest son, me, into care in the first instance. I have used the term "forced" to demonstrate that he clearly had no alternative. It was impossible for him to hold down a job and care for his four children at the same time. It was an inevitability that as a baby I would need nursing as well as caring and I was admitted into the Boys Garden City at Woodford Bridge on the 3rd April 1947. Our father was able to cope alone with Francis, George and John until 21st April 1947 when they were reunited with me at Woodford Bridge.

Well that's what happened to us and I guess the same fate was inflicted upon many children who grew up in similarly unfortunate circumstances in post-war Britain of the 1950s. It seems strange that the situation that had befallen my parents could have had such a devastating impact upon their children. In the blink of an eye a decision was made and our journey through life was suddenly changed forever. Were we heading for unsafe and unchartered waters? Was it to be for the better or the worse? I leave it for you to decide!

Aims - But how's it to be done?

I make no bones about the fact that I was never a child prodigy and, surprising as it might seem, I was unable to read or write when I entered Barnardo's care. After all I was only six months old. As a consequence my earliest "memories" of our lives together were, in fact, those imparted to me by my siblings. My own earliest and personal recollections were when I was about three years of age and living in Somerset.

I was always grateful that we remained together for most of the time and were able to look out for each other when the need arose. It was also a unique situation to have four siblings together at one time in one home. The photograph (below), was probably taken at Woodford Bridge when we were reunited. Barnardo's were sticklers for photographing and recording every aspect of our growth and development while we were in their care. This picture shows us as we entered into care together with George and John (top left and right) and myself and Francis (lower right).

In tackling our story it was never my intention that it would be a day to day account of life in an institution. My aim here is to describe the many memories and anecdotes that we had the pleasure of enjoying and sharing together as four young siblings that found themselves living in an alien environment.

Over the years it was always on the cards that one or another of us would eventually get down to writing an account of our lives and experiences. In this account it is my intention to describe the pivotal events that impacted us as a very close knit "band of brothers". This makes the experiences unique to us and therefore worthy of exploration and dissemination. In addition I am also very conscious that the narrative is intimate, in that it is describing aspects of our young lives in all their innocent naivety. Therefore my aim is to ensure that narrative will seek to describe the events in our lives with poignancy and truthfulness.

So be prepared to be drawn into our adventures together and

occasionally to learn our unusual Barnardo lingo. Share in the disappointments when visitors failed to turn up and the pathos felt from reunions; my meeting a new uncle who was to become a "dad" for the first time and oh! I also nearly forgot, a new "brother" for the first time.

I have three reasons for deciding to take the task on for myself:

Firstly, we, my brothers and I, are all "getting on a bit". I am now in my seventies and I want to put my memories down on paper while I am still able.

Secondly, there were only a handful of children in care who could boast that they had elder siblings in the same home. This automatically placed us all up the pecking order and ensured that we were able to command the utmost respect from other lads in our dormitories. Also as well as protecting each other our situation provided us with an unparalleled opportunity to make the most of our times together. So, despite being away from a real home environment, we actually had much to be grateful for. Collectively we were able to exploit the shortcomings, of an institutional life, and together really make the most of the situation that we were in.

Finally, in this account are descriptions of events and happenings that would now be classed as historic and of the times. In fact they are of great social significance. These events took place when the ethos of child care still had its roots in final vestiges of the Victorian model of child care. Fortunately, over the ensuing years, ideas regarding child welfare have been challenged and changed for the "better". The notion of placing children into vast inhospitable mansions was recognised, long ago, as unacceptable. Now the care model seems to want to provide an authentic home-style environment for children with a mother and father figurehead rather than of nurse or a matron.

I have now made clear my aims for this book. I hope that it will make for some entertaining reading and that there will be something for everybody including the three letter word that begins with S and ends with an X. I think now is the time to proceed. So sit back, enjoy and let the adventures commence as our life in care unfolds.

CHAPTER ONE

The seaside, a legacy, smugglers and a teddy

For we four brothers, ranging in age from six months to seven years, our lives would never be the same again and were just about to change forever. Whether that was for better or for worse will always be open to debate. For us the consequences of our time in care was to become very evident when we were older and when we eventually met our extended family members for the first time.

Fortunately being allowed to remain together meant that it was inevitable that opportunities for some lively goings-on would take place over the ensuing years. That is precisely what happened and what better place to start our adventure than in Ashley Coombe, a mansion situated high on the edge of an Exmoor hillside in Somerset (above).

One of my earliest recollections of life at Ashley Coombe, almost certainly assisted by brotherly inputs and adult visits, was the outstanding beauty of its surroundings. Nestled within woodland, above Worthy, the house had extensive uninterrupted views across Porlock bay, the Bristol Channel and across the bay was the South coast of Wales. The view, taken below, was taken from the lawns of Ashley Coombe and represents the view that we saw every day.

In later years I was to discover the cultural history and importance of Ashley Coombe including the important legacy that its earliest owners were to bestow upon the world of contemporary technology. It was Lord King, the 8th Baron and 1st Earl of Lovelace who improved and extended the house as well as creating the tiered Italianate gardens that can be seen in the picture (above). The house, built in the style of an Italian castle, was accessed through the woods, via several tunnels and walled walkways, which led from the beach area up into the Coombe itself. The tunnels were certainly large enough to accommodate a man on horseback or a horse and gig and in several of the routes they were large enough for motor vehicles to approach the house unseen (below).

In 1835 a certain Lord King married Augusta Ada Byron, the daughter of the English poet, peer and politician Lord Bryon and they made Ashley Coombe their home. Ada Lovelace was a mathematician, writer and renowned for her work on Charles Babbage's mechanical computer. It was Ada who made the initial discovery that the machine had applications way beyond just carrying out pure calculations. She later went on to publish, what was effectively, the prototype algorithm to function and interface with the machine. Today Ada's legacy and contribution in the field of mathematics, computing and computer programming are highly regarded.

Ashley Combe house was eventually let to Barnardo's as a children's home in 1939; however, by 1950 the site was considered unsafe as a children's home. The children, including us, had to be relocated elsewhere throughout the UK but I will come to that later on. For a short period the house became a country club; however gained a somewhat disreputable reputation locally. Sadly the house was abandoned and fell into disrepair. The structure and foundations of the house had become irretrievably destabilised by soil and land movements over the years and it was finally demolished in 1974. Today there is nothing remaining to indicate that such a majestic house was ever present at that particular site and sadly the Porlock connection with Ada Lovelace was lost and gone forever.

As we settled into life at Ashley Coombe the bond between my brother, Francis, and myself intensified and I became more clingy and reliant upon him. We shared a dormitory with the other younger boys whilst my two older siblings, George and John, slept in the older boy's dorm. Over the coming months Francis would look after me and protect me from anyone who thought that they might take a pop at the "Tyrrells".

The day to day routine in Ashley Coombe was quite regimented which meant that we always had to be appropriately attired. For example we had to wear approved "indoor" clothing for all activities like breakfast, or for indoor playtime otherwise "outdoor" clothing was the norm. The regime also included having to sit at the dining table with our clean hands under our knees and there was definitely little or no talking until we were told to.

That was the day to day routine, as I remember it, with no deviation.

Life for the older boys was somewhat different to ours. For instance on Sunday mornings they were permitted to walk through the Yearnor Woods to St. Beuno's Church, in Culbone, for Sunday worship. In addition for some of the older boys, like John who had started school, a taxi would collect them each morning and drive them down to Porlock village where the Junior School was located. In contrast we youngsters were never allowed out of the sight of our carers. I guess, on the whole, I did not move far from the house and its immediate grounds the whole time I was living there.

It was during this time that Francis began to fill our young heads, that is the younger boys in the "babe's dorm", with tales of swashbucklers, pirates and smugglers. Some of the older boys had been reading adventure books, in particular, Treasure Island and Robinson Crusoe and would play act by pretending to have a peg-leg and they would walk around saying "Ah Jim lad". They definitely inspired Francis with their tales of adventure. It was also easy to see how the local views would also have stimulated him as one could clearly see Porlock Weir, just down from the Coombe, and the Bristol Channel was right in front of us with views of Wales. Every day we would look at the ships sailing along the channel and the boats coming to and fro in the harbour. Yes, we loved living by the seaside even though I didn't get much of a chance to enjoy it at that time as I was too young.

I enjoyed the tales that Francis related and I felt that he was really getting into his stride with the other boys sitting on the floor, in a ring, around him and listening intently. Sometimes they would make appropriate noises when they felt fearful or would shout out "*get the police*" if the smugglers became too tasty. Two things, however, really worried me.

Firstly, I wasn't too sure what to make of swashbucklers and pirates other than they didn't carry out their activities in the Bristol Channel as far as I knew. Or did they?

Secondly, and much more worrying for me, was that the smugglers were local men who lived just down the hill in Porlock Weir. This was very close to home. Furthermore, according to Francis, they would routinely use our tunnels, the tunnels in the grounds of Ashley Coombe, to secrete their ill-gotten gains, such as rum. If that wasn't bad enough Francis reckoned that the smugglers actually hid their booty somewhere in the grounds of Ashley Coombe. He told us that under no circumstances were we to make any mention of this to the staff as the leader, the notorious Mr Tyke, an infamous smuggler, knew us all and would come looking for us. This was our secret and our secret only. Nobody was to divulge his secret as Mr Tyke would know!

Well, I was both hooked by the excitement of it all and yet fearful that I might encounter the frightful Mr Tyke who thought nothing of making little boys "disappear" into thin air if they ever "snitched" on him. I became convinced that I needed to keep an eye out for him, possibly under the misguided notion that I, alone, could safeguard us all, and so this became a pattern of events in our dorm over the next few weeks.

Although I wasn't too sure exactly what it was that I was looking out for, or what it was that I might find, my boldness and purpose gave me esteem and respect within the dorm. I liked the feeling of power that I had suddenly acquired and, although I was still only two and half, it was Mr Tyke who was to keep me on my toes for the foreseeable future. It is clear that my brother had made a convincing case for the presence of the smugglers. In the meantime I became even more convinced that I could hear them getting up to their skulduggery in the woods. I made it my business to keep "obbos" at the window looking and listening for any movement or rustling that would tell me that Tyke was about. With my "pluto" torch in my hand, teddy up close to my face and Francis asleep in his bed close-by I felt very safe doing my duty for the boys.

One evening teddy and I decided that we needed to use the chamber pot before we began our nightly watch. At that time of the evening, however, with over ten boys in the dorm the potty was not a pretty sight. Nevertheless I dipped teddy into the pot so that he could do "what comes naturally to a young teddy bear" and when I pulled him out again I have to admit he stank and was very wet. I think that I had immersed him too far!

As it was highly improbable that teddy would need to use the potty again, that night, I decided that we should retire to bed in spite of the state that he was in. My brother thought it all a jolly jape and was laughing his head off as he saw me grab teddy from the potty and take him to bed still wet from his dipping. This was all too much for me and my bear and as we were both sleepy we soon forgot about Tyke and his dirty deeds. Whatever the smugglers got up to on that night was of no interest to me! The next morning I took teddy to the dormitory nurse who gave him a jolly good washing for me. When I returned from breakfast I saw him hanging by his ear from the clothes line. For the next few days I only had wolly to keep me company as teddy underwent a deep cleaning. A few days later we were reunited and I felt very happy, as at last we could resume our nightly duties on-guard looking for Tyke. Unfortunately, I don't really know why, but it was always in my mind that this task was unsuitable for wolly who remained, on watch, propped against my pillow throughout the nightly vigil.

A day or so after teddy got his soaking Francis with a real "strop" on, and feeling particularly "urdy" and agitated. He was looking for someone to vent his feelings upon. It was sometime before I realised the reason why he was feeling the way that he was but in the meantime he happened to focus his anger upon me and teddy. Fortunately wolly got off "Scott free". It was later in the morning, before breakfast, when I noticed that teddy was absent from his pride of place on the window sill watching over his terrain. I looked to Francis for an explanation and all he would say was that I was far too old for a teddy, that he was now unhygienic and far too dirty and smelly. Under the circumstances he had personally made the decision that teddy should go.

I was shocked to the core and remember being beside myself with grief and very concerned about how I might continue my nightly sentinel duties without teddy's help. Later on I went to John to seek his support and told him of how Francis had pinched teddy and wouldn't give him back to me. I was hoping that he would have taken my side and given me the reassurances and comfort that was needed. Although, at that time, I never knew the mystery of Francis's bad mood it appeared that John also had it too. I wondered whether it was catching and whether I might also become terribly "urdy" like them.

Much to my surprise and dismay John actually agreed with Francis that I was too old for a teddy. He claimed that it made me look like a cissy boy and that cissy boys would not be tolerated in his gang. That if

I wanted to continue as a member of his gang, then no teddies! Just to put me firmly in my place he then clipped me behind the ear, told me to stop crying as I was grown up now and to get on with my breakfast.

That was true Barnardo justice for you.

When I returned to my dorm I looked from the window and to my utter joy I saw teddy lying face down in the mud. I couldn't wait to get him and asked the master if I could leave, dressed as I was, to retrieve him. I never let on to Francis or John that I had found him in the back garden and that I had I retrieved him, washed him down and kept him in my locker. Unfortunately teddy never publicly resurfaced again and I could only have a cuddle with him when I was either on my own in the dorm or when everybody else was asleep. I was a day older but it seemed longer and I was feeling just as teddy looked crest-fallen and sad!

Training (Ashley Coombe style), panic in the woods and a meeting

Each morning, while the older boys were at school, the children from "babes" dorm received an equally important but slightly different kind of education, namely, potty training. This important activity was carried out on a daily basis until we were all "fit for purpose" in that department.

Like most activities in Barnardo's our training was executed with military precision. With a home full of children it made sense that such a delicate activity would take place en masse. This would be of particular importance if the children were to go visiting as a group or if they were to attend a local church service.

The training commenced punctually at the same time every day, that was, just after we had eaten breakfast and carried out our daily chores. Typically the nurse would escort the "babes" to the potty room where there was a line of chamber pots. We were then told to sit down on the potty until we had been successful in carrying out the task in hand. Once the feat had been accomplished we let nurse know, by clapping our hands, and that we were ready for the next step. The nurse would then help us to clean and dress before hand-washing took place. Only after we had fulfilled all of these steps were we allowed to go outside to play on the lawns until we were called back for indoor play time. Playing out was very important to me and so it was no surprise that I was always one of the first children to let out potty room and out onto the playing field.

I can remember one particular incident that occurred one Sunday morning that left me in an utter state of panic and fear. I really thought that my time had come! It happened when the older boys had gone off to attend the service at our local church in Culbone. The walk to the church took the boys deep into the woodlands along very uneven gravel pathways and up and down through the woodland ravines. It was considered to be too far, too long and too demanding for us younger ones. The church itself is very special as it is said to be the smallest parish church in England and dedicated to the Welsh Saint Bueno. I have to say that I had never ventured into the woods before. I found them to be very spooky, full of strange noises, rustlings, crackling twigs and grotesque gnarled trees.

Despite having a nurse to accompany us I was, nevertheless, still quite scared and was full of trepidations. In particular I had concerns about the smugglers and whether we might cross their path, and of course, there was Mr. Tyke still carrying out his foul deeds. Worst still, in spite of the other children and the nurse, I nonetheless felt unsafe and lonely without my brothers or teddy for support and protection.

As we ventured deeper into the woods my confidence grew and I actually began to enjoy myself but for some reason, or another, I still remained some distance from the main group of children. All seemed to be going well and our journey was uneventful when suddenly, and to my horror, I realised that someone or something had hold of my left ankle. I just could not move it, I was stuck and the more I tried to free myself by pulling at the mystical grip around my ankle the tighter it became. It was now beginning to hurt me and I was scared when I suddenly realised that I was in deep trouble. The sheer fear and panic, that engulfed any limited rational thoughts that I may have had, were gone and I just began to cry and wail very, very loudly. My worst fears were now coming true as the nurse and the other children continued on their walk without me. I wasn't even being missed by them and there I was, stranded alone in the woods, with a hideous creature holding me down by my ankle and preventing my escape. I was so terrified I just couldn't bring myself to look down to see what the cause was. Panic had now taken over the very essence of my behaviour and understanding and I even convinced myself that the gentle summer breeze had now turned into a full scale wind screaming through the tree tops and howling like a banshee and calling out to me "we've got you now little nipper Ha! Ha! Ha!"

"That's it", I decided, "there was no escape from this"! As the children became just a dot on the horizon I concluded that I was now in the claws of the dastardly Tyke.

My screaming and crying had, however, been sufficient to alert the nurse who rapidly returned to save me. She was frantic with worry and all the other children rallied around to free my leg from what, in fact, was a poacher's snare. I wasn't too sure what such a device was or why it was on the path that I was treading on or what a poacher was but, to be quite honest, I didn't care. I was just glad to be free of it and able to resume my walk with the others. As far as I and my brothers were concerned this was a very real and close encounter with the King of Smugglers, Mr Tyke, and I couldn't wait to tell Francis.

On our return from the walk there were, yet again, another set of rules that we had to follow. Firstly, we all had to go to the wash room to clean our hands and then walk along to the boot room to clean our Wellington boots. Then once we had carried out these duties we were duly inspected by a master and if we passed them we would then be permitted to place our boots in the correct boot rack. I had my own boot space allocation in the cloak room with my name, William, emblazoned above it. Woe betide any boy who decided to put his boots in my allotted space. Personal spaces, in Ashley Coombe, was rare and so any area allocated to us individually was guarded and protected by us as though our lives depended upon it. Eventually having carried out these chores we were allowed to go upstairs to be re-acquainted with the older boys and my brothers. I just couldn't wait to tell them of my most frightening experience in the woods.

As I recited my tale of sheer horror to them all I sensed that it was not being received in the way that I had anticipated. I was expecting cuddles and words of comfort and praise for my bravery. Alas this was not to be. As far as they were concerned I was just being a wimp and should never have cried in the way I did in public. They reckoned that I had let the "Tyrrells" down and that they might slip from grace and esteem as a result of my childish behaviour. Worst still, as far as John was concerned, I needed a jolly good slapping. His rhetoric, however, was part of his leadership bravado and secretly, when the others were not looking, he slipped his hand in mine and squeezed it lovingly.

That was the good side of life in Barnardo's with my brothers by my side giving me support.

It was shortly after my incident in the woods that I was finally told the reason why my brother's had been so beastly to me and why they were so sullen with everybody else. They were feeling unsettled by the news that had recently been shared with them. According to John the reason that he was acting like a rotter was because our mother, whoever she was, had made contact with the Barnardo's family liaison team to request permission to visit us. He had been informed of this by matron. John, who was then nearly ten years of age, still harboured vivid memories of the fights and arguments between our parents back in Walthamstow, long before the eventual break-up of the family unit.

John was the piggy in the middle and he reckoned that home life had become a disaster area with shouting, throwing of crockery and screaming. In fact he said that our mother's behaviour was even more volatile! He went on to say that our being taken in by Barnardo's was a lifeline and that we were better off there than back in Walthamstow.

In contrast life at Ashley Coombe was stable, settled and peaceful. We enjoyed regular meals and although not always my favourite choice, they nonetheless filled the gap and were satisfying. John told me that he especially liked the tranquility of life beside the sea and the continuity that our life in Barnardo's brought to us. The routineness and predictability of our day to day life was so much more refreshing than the random and chaotic life that we lived in Walthamstow. He said that you never knew when you might eat or whether you would be able to get some sleep away from the rows. Now, free of the arguments and bickering, John enjoyed a certain level of esteem and respect from the other boys and his "father-figure" role for his siblings. Much later on I remember him saying that they were some of the best days of his life.

It was made abundantly clear to me, from John's exposé of life with our parents, why the prospect of any kind of reunion or the faintest hint of any form of repatriation filled him with anxiety and horror. Inevitably his disdain of such a notion filtered down to George and Francis and hence his recent "urdiness" with me.

To be honest, I could not see what the fuss was all about as I had absolutely no idea what this all meant. Although I had obviously heard of mothers and seen pictures of a mother in books and in my comics; I had no reality of what they were or of their day to day role. We had nurses who looked after us but they were not my mother, they were nurses, so why the fuss? John, George and Francis were my "parents" and that was all I needed and all I wanted. I certainly had no idea who she was or what to expect of her, if or when, we were formally introduced to her again.

In the meantime, as the dust and the excitement began to settle down again, Francis and I resumed our play time together at every opportunity. I have to admit that without teddy, to participate in my nightly vigils, my interest in Mr Tyke and his misdemeanours was beginning to wane and fade from view. We now had a new distraction in our lives in the form of a big red London bus that, together, we drove around the lawns of Ashley Coombe. In fact it wasn't a bus at all; it was the steering wheel of the bus. It came in the form of a large steel wheel, located on the edge of the front lawn, that controlled the sluice gate which in turn regulated the water supply to the various tiered water garden features (see next page). For us, however, it was the steering wheel of a London bus.

To be honest with you, I didn't really know what role a bus served. I assumed that everybody on the "outside" lived like us and if you couldn't walk to your destination through Worthy Woods one would telephone Mr. Jones for a taxi. Francis, on the other hand, knew all about them as he had seen an illustration of a bus in a book about Transport of England in the playroom library. At this stage in his life it would be true to say that he was an obsessive about buses and had mastered all of the appropriate noises. Thus he could mimic the sound of the engine and the clicking noise of the bus ticket being clipped. However his pièce de résistance was the request that the conductor made to the passengers which went something like "aaanymoore farrres pleeease" and said in a weird whining voice that only Francis could make!!

He dominated the wheel when we were playing in the gardens and woe betide anybody who went near it or, come to that, anybody that even thought that they might approach it. The wheel was his territory and he would defend it to the last. Life continued on as usual and John and George seemed to be in a better frame of mind. Frank was still defending his right to the sole ownership and use of the steel wheel, and Mr Tyke? Well I guess that I had outgrown him. As teddy was now relegated to my locker and out of sight I came to the conclusion that so was My Tyke and his band of smugglers. The fun had gone, to be replaced by bus driving, and as the saying goes "out of mind, out of sight". I was a big boy now; in fact, I was training to be a substitute bus conductor and was now able to make the ping-ping noise that the ticket machine made. I reckoned that I had now arrived!

On one particular occasion, while John and George were at school, a rather unusual occurrence took place. In hindsight the events of this memorable day represented the very beginning of the end of our lives in the care of Barnardo Homes. Francis and I were playing on the front lawns, as usual, and getting ready to resume our bus duties together when one of the nurses came running from the house, calling out our names. She was quite breathless and was shouting out that she needed to speak to us about an urgent matter. This was a very unusual scenario and one that we had never faced before. We both wondered what it was that we may have done to cause such a reaction!

In my naivety I began to recite to Francis the entire list of the morning's "things-to-be-done" list just to see in case one or the other of us had omitted anything.

"Had he", I asked, "done his chores, eaten all of his breakfast, cleaned his plate away, cleared the table, done one for the pot, washed his hands, got into play clothes, and lastly, asked Sir for permission to play".

Well we had done everything that was expected of us and so with clear consciences we gingerly approached the nurse.

"Francis and William", she said, "You need to get out of your play clothes, put on your outside clothes and meet me in the playroom forthwith".

We looked at each other and simply responded with the question "Why"? By now she was very agitated and was almost glowing with anger for us keeping her waiting and for our disobedience.

She then informed us that we had a visitor who was waiting to see us and before we asked, "No, John and George will not be returning from school especially" and "they will have to wait for another day!" We simply shrugged our shoulders and did what we were told to do and marched back to our dorm. By the time we had changed and assembled in the playroom there was much speculation as to who might be visiting us.

I wondered whether it might be the Queen. She had featured a lot in the newspapers and on the radio and she was one of my favourite women of all time. In fact apart from the nurses she was the only woman that I knew about. Francis, on the other hand, thought it might be the doctor coming to see us.

I asked him "why would he need to come as neither of us was ill"

He replied that "he was probably coming along to make us cough like he does with the older boys. After all George and John said that he did that with them and to all of the older boys".

I was a bit perplexed by his answer and as I stood around wondering why the doctor would want the boys to cough the nurse came into the playroom and asked us to join Sir on the front lawn. To my surprise the lawn was clear of children and wondered what could have been so important that they would be confined to the house.

Sir approached us to inform us that we had a very special visitor and he ushered us forward just as a lady appeared from behind a bush.

"This," said Sir, "is your mother. Come now, say hello to her".

We looked at each other with puzzled expressions on our faces and not too sure exactly how to respond. I remember wishing that John was with us as he would know what to do. Francis seemed reticent and was somewhat reluctant to make the first move. I had no such reservations: she was simply a woman like our cook, matron or the Vicar's wife and so I stepped forward with my hand held out and shook her hand saying "Hello Madam". Although we were told that she was my mother this meant nothing to me. Her acquaintanceship to me was of no more importance than the next person that I was never going to meet again. She was a stranger and I felt nothing for her. As Sir left us alone to chat together we suddenly realised that she was not alone. From behind a tree came a man who was introduced to us as Uncle Bill.

To me, this man looked strange as he was wearing his jacket on back to front and that was very odd. It was at that precise moment when the penny dropped and I realised that Francis and I were victims of the worst form of skulduggery. In fact the impact was so shocking that I began to cry as we were now in the presence of the dentist as it is only the dentist that wears his coat back to front! Clearly this was some new ploy that Sir was using to get the younger boys, especially the more cautious ones, to see the dentist. To me everything fitted perfectly. As far as I was concerned if he looked like a dentist and wore the uniform of a dentist then he probably was the dentist.

My feelings soon impacted Francis who also started to wail very loudly. We hadn't said much to either of them. However our crying had alerted Sir, who came running back to us to see what all of the commotion was about. Although the regime at the home was strict and run along the lines of the military it was the children that came first and any indication that they were suffering or were unhappy was treated very seriously. Sir was obviously very concerned over our disposition and our response to meeting these strangers. Although I was blubbering I managed to explain to Sir just how we were both feeling as I told him "that we did not want to see the dentist today and that we would much rather be permitted to return to our dorm".

Once in our dorm we both sat on the edges of our bed wondering what on earth that was all about. I remember thinking that teddy would help to console me if only I could. In the meantime, however, I had to put up with Francis. Later that day we had a meeting with Sir who confirmed that the man was definitely an uncle, called Bill, and not the dentist. He told us that he had worn his outer coat in that way to protect himself from the wind as they had travelled all the way from London to Porlock on a motorbike.

Whether our mother had deliberately misled the Barnardo's Family Unit into thinking that Bill Beavis was, in fact, our father we shall never know. To me this very brief meeting was a non-event, a tearful and frightening non-event, but nevertheless it really meant nothing to me. Furthermore I was pleased that I did not have any dental treatment that day. Francis, as usual, was non-committal about his thoughts and feelings of the day. In fact, he has always rather preferred to keep his cards close to his chest. Anyway; the excitement for the day was over, the meeting was brief and now behind us and it was time for tea with our brothers. As far as we were concerned that was the end of the matter and any thoughts of being repatriated, whatever that meant, soon became a distant memory.

Storm clouds, however, were gathering on the horizon! There were important changes and separations looming but, for us, ignorance was bliss and in the meantime it was our time to be together. As Francis and I excitedly related the story to John and George I got the distinct feeling that they were both rather pleased with the outcome, especially the way that things turned out for our Mother and this man. Just who did they think they were, coming down to our home, out of the blue, after nearly three years and disrupting the status quo in the way that they had! We were really happy that it was over but our contentedness was soon to be challenged yet again and the security that we were enjoying was to be pulled from under our feet.

Unsettling times, a move and a tearful goodbye to teddy and wolly

As it happened our time at Ashley Coombe was never going to be long term. For a start John and George were too old to remain there as it was really only suitable for babes, toddlers and younger ones. Certainly not strapping young lads that they were now both becoming. Also the house itself was considered to becoming unsafe and unfit for purpose.

The main problem centred upon the unstable environment on which the home was built. We had observed that the pathways through Yearnor and Worthy Woods had become increasingly unsafe due to landslides. Several of the public pathways had been deemed too unsafe and were closed to the public and the famous tunnels, from the Weir to Ashley Coombe, were now considered too precarious for the public to walk through. In addition the traditional and direct route from Ashley Coombe to Culbone Church had disappeared in a landslide. A new path was quickly constructed, uphill from the old one, however with the necessary diversions it added about a further mile or so to the journey. This made the boys' Sunday worship at Culbone Church almost impossible by foot from Ashley Coombe due to the distance and the rugged terrain that they would encounter on the new route. In time the unstable nature of the Coombe began to impact directly upon structural integrity of Ashley Coombe itself.

Previously Lord Lytton, the owner of Ashley Coombe, had complained to the Barnardo's authorities about the vast amount of water that was being consumed by the home. He made the suggestion that the children bathe communally and then he took it upon himself to ration the amount available for the home to use.

One consequence of this action was that the beautiful lawn, a great feature of the house, began to wither and dry out in places. Over time large cracks began to appear in the lawn and we were prevented from playing out on it. Within months of the water rationing the stone Italianate walls began to crumble and fall away and within the house, itself, large cracks suddenly appeared on the south facing walls. The "final nail in the coffin" came when one day one of our bedroom windows, along with the framework, just cracked all by itself.

It really came as no surprise to us when we were told that our days at Ashley Coombe were drawing to a close and that we would have to be relocated to a safer and more hospitable environment. I have to say that, with great sadness and a heavy heart, I could understand the decision and, to be quite frank, the sooner the better for us all.

Ashley Coombe, the old lady of Porlock and the jewel of Yearnor Wood, had served Barnardo's well but it was now time for both Barnardo's and the Tyrrell brothers to move on to pastures new. God Bless Ashley Coombe and all who served within her beautiful grounds and buildings. We enjoyed our time living there and the brotherly bond that was formed though our coalescence was to remain throughout our adulthood. Yes it would be true to say that for me, who knew no other form of existence other than Ashley Coombe, our lives living in the old lady in the woods was enjoyable and I remain truly grateful that we shared the experience together.

The house has remained indelibly imprinted in my memory and in adulthood our frequent pilgrimages to Porlock Weir would always include a walk to the Toll Road in search of, what remains of, the service road to the house. Just a gate and a path remain but the molecules of my childhood will remain there for evermore. Even today as I stare at the space where the house once stood I can't help but doff my cap in her direction. My very first return to the house took place in the late 1960s when it was still intact but in a very distressed state. When I returned with my wife in the early seventies it had all but disappeared under the undergrowth and only a few vestiges of the once majestic building remained such as the garden gallery (below).

For us, still living in Ashley Combe, it was a bit of a waiting game and over the next few days we all waited in anticipation to see what was to become of us. Shortly afterwards the big day arrived and one morning the nurse came to the dorm, extra early, to wake us up. She barked at us to pack all of our belongings into one bag only.

She told us that "if you can't get your stuff in the bag provided you'll have to leave it behind".

We were then told to put on our "outdoor" clothes, have breakfast and meet under the clock by 9 a.m.

"This is it," said Francis. "We are leaving and going on a journey".

As he spoke to me I realised that I was facing a real dilemma, one great big pickle, and no matter how hard I tried I knew that I was going to have to make the ultimate sacrifice and Francis refused to help me out. The major problem that I encountered was no matter how hard I tried I just could not get both teddy and wolly into my bag with all of my other belongings and clothes. My "pluto" torch and catapult had absolute priority but I discovered that if I left either my Wellingtons or my plimsolls and dungarees out of the bag I could accommodate both teddy and wolly.

The thought of leaving my friends and comforters behind filled me with the worst case of sadness imaginable. The alternative, the prospect of getting the cane for leaving my boots or dungarees behind, soon made me come to my senses. It was with the greatest of regret that both of my lifelong buddies were to remain abandoned, forlorn and left alone in my locker. Despite being almost an adult now, I was nearly four after all, and I still couldn't let the event pass without sobbing my heart out. I was sure going to miss my little furry friends.

For me this seemed to be an even greater wrench than leaving Ashley Coombe itself. Even the excitement of embarking upon the next chapter of our lives did little to console me at that time. However, I have to admit that, secretly, I was looking forward to the next stage of our lives together. Previously Francis and I had been told by John and George that our next move would be to Marford's, another big country house, in Bromborough, Cheshire.

Anyway that is what Francis and I were led to believe!

CHAPTER TWO

If this isn't Marfords then where are we?

In the summer of 1949 our time living and being cared for at Ashley Coombe finally came to an end. Initially John and George left for Marfords. Francis and I became upset at being parted from them however one of the younger nurses was very reassuring and informed us that it made sense for the older boys to go ahead of us. As it happened we left to join them just a few days later.

All ten of us, the very youngsters, along with the nurse and a travelling matron were taken by taxi to Minehead Station to catch a train. For me this journey was different. It wasn't exciting and it didn't have the feel of a pleasure trip, like a holiday, and it wasn't exciting like a shopping trip. I remember feeling remorseful and lonely as I looked over my shoulder, through the taxi window, at my old home disappearing into the distance and out of sight. Little did I know that I would never see the house in its majestic glory again! Good bye teddy! Good bye Wolly

The next thing I remember was the train pulling into a station somewhere else and it was dark and I was tired. Fortunately for us we were met from the train by a bus that took us directly to the home. Despite our fatigue, from the long journey, Francis and I were very anxious to be reunited with our older brothers. It's funny but we both felt insecure in their absence, sort of incomplete. Under the circumstances, without them around for support, we both decided that it would be best to keep our mouths well and truly shut and our opinions to ourselves. On our arrival there was a welcoming committee who showed us to our dormitory. We were then told to change and wash and then meet in the dining room for supper. I may have been shattered but I liked my food; I wasn't called Tubs for nothing you know. At supper Francis whispered to me that he thought it funny that when we arrived he didn't hear them say welcome to Marfords. He was sure that they mentioned another name but we were both too sleepy to have either noticed this or even cared.

I just wanted my supper and then bed.

It was just as we were tucking-in to supper that Francis mentioned that all of the boys were like us, babes and toddlers, and that in fact there were no big boys in the hall at all. What's more George and John were nowhere in sight. We mentioned this to one of the other boys on our table who incidentally hadn't travelled with us from Ashley Coombe. I was really very surprised by his demeanour as his hands and finger nails were filthy, his hair was uncombed and he seemed to be ill-prepared for sitting at the table especially as we just about to start to eat. I was so flabbergasted that I made a point of telling Francis of this as well. Whether the boy heard my criticism or not I wasn't too sure however he had obviously taken an instant dislike to us.

He looked across at us and sneeringly told us to "Shut up new boys or you'll get a slapping".

By now we were both very tired and upset at our plight. It was time for bed. It was good that all the boys went to bed at the same time just as we had done at Ashley Coombe. As I began to doze off all I could think about was what I was going to tell John and George in the morning about our adventures on the train journey.

As I quietly mimicked the chuff, chuff whoo! whoo! of the steam train I had spent my first night at Marfords. Or had I?

The next morning we assembled for breakfast and as we entered the dining room we noticed that, yet again, it was only the toddlers and babes eating. Francis asked a different person where the older boys were. We were both expecting the child to tell us something along the lines that the older boys have breakfast earlier than us so that they can be ready for school, work or what have you. Just as they did at Ashley Coombe.

His response shocked us when he told us that this home was just like "Babes Castle" in that only babes and toddlers lived here.

"But what about our older brothers? They are supposed to be here with us at Marfords, Francis replied". "Where are they then?"

The lad told us that "he didn't have a clue where they were and that incidentally, he didn't know what Marfords were, but whatever it was this place ain't it".

After breakfast we asked to see matron about an important matter and sat in the hall waiting for her. We were ushered into her office whereupon she asked us a string of standard but nevertheless rather odd questions.

"What was wrong with us? Were we suffering from anything? Had we eaten our prunes? How was our first night?

Well Francis just looked at her and asked of her where our brothers were as we could not find them. She left us for a minute or so and then returned with an old man on tow, who we presumed was the new Sir.

He asked us "what all the fuss was about and then informed us that John and George had settled down in Marfords, in Bromborough.

Francis told Sir "that was not true because we were at Marfords". Then the penny dropped and we realised that we had been separated despite being told that all of us were to remain together as a family unit in one place. That was what we were told before we left Ashley Coombe and that was the great hope that we were holding on to.

"Look Francis", said Sir, "This isn't Marfords". That particular home is for boys from seven to eleven years of age and you are both too young. This is Charlton Park (above) and it is for babes and toddlers like you both. You will have to get used to the idea that you will be here for the foreseeable future. Now toddle off and be good boys. We don't want any sort of trouble here do we?"

We left the matron's office in tears and in desperate need of the kind of reassurances that only our brothers, or my long lost furry friends could have provided.

William hatches a plan, a bully and a reunion.

As it was now our play-time we decided to sit by ourselves in the garden and consider our next plan of action, perhaps, to even hatch a strategy for us all to be reunited. Frank's initial thought was that we should run away. I gave this some serious thought but after at least five seconds of serious contemplation and deep consideration I realised that I hated the idea of not having any food "on tap". In addition to this we really had no idea where we were and so we quickly abandoned that notion.

He then suggested that we might recruit a nurse to write a letter to John and George asking them to either, come and see us, or to write to us. However, we both concluded that we could not trust any of them to write down precisely what we wanted her to say on our behalf. It was then that I had a brilliant brainwave and came up with a sure winner of an idea.

I had many talents and by exploiting my most accomplished skill I was convinced that we would eventually get our own way. It was my intention that I would wait until we were all assembled together in the dining room for breakfast before I carried it out. My plan was that I would march down to the master bench and then hold my breath in front of all of the staff on the front table until they yielded and returned us to our brothers. I was particularly good at holding my breath and Francis reckoned that I was champion at it and not even the big boys could beat me. The more I thought about this, the more I became convinced that it would work. I had used this before as a way of getting my own way. In general I didn't have to wait too long before people responded. The sight of a young boy with ballooning cheeks, like a howler monkey, bulging eyes, like golf balls on a tee and a crimson complexion soon made them respond. Yes, I thought, that would definitely do the trick.

Much to my disappointment Francis thought that this was a terrible idea and doomed to failure. I asked him to explain himself, after all, he had previously told me that I was one of the best at breath holding even better than Houdini, whoever he was! In truth, and this is the hard bit, he reckoned that I wasn't that good at all and he was just trying to cheer me up by telling me that I was good at something. I was really angry with him and decided that I would show him what for and then I went for it. As my cheeks began to bellow out Francis simply closed my nostrils with his finger and thumb and I soon started to cough and inhale.

"Why did you do that for, you rotter?" I said.

"Tubs you idiot, you were breathing in all the time. You really are a terrible breath-holder. We need to come up with another plan that doesn't involve you looking like a complete and utter moron," replied Francis.

"It's not fair", I said. "You always poo-hoo my ideas. Why don't you get on with it on your own"? At that I sloped away further down into the gardens and out of his sight.

I hadn't gone too far when I bumped into the objectionable boy at our supper table the night before.

I said "Hello," and he told me "to shut it new boy," or he would bash me up.

I told him that "I thought he was a rotter and that if he had been in Ashley Coombe the nurse would have pulled him by his ear lobe to the washroom to wash his dirty hands and finger nails and give his hair a jolly good combing".

I am not too sure what happened next but I was sitting on my bottom and I started to cry. Just at that moment Francis joined us and the boy looked at him and said.

"Do you want some as well new boy? Do you want a bashing too? I am only too happy to oblige. You twerp?"

Well, I thought, we are in for it now. However Francis came up with a real humdinger of a get-out clause.

"Listen", said Francis," "While we were at Ashley Coombe Sir put a sixpenny saving stamp away for us every week. Mine still had five bob in it and if you promise to leave us alone you can have it all".

To my utter amazement the boy agreed to Francis's proposal, on a hand shake, and we were never threatened again. As it happened the boy never saw the savings book or any of the money. To this day I have never really understood why it was that the boy failed to take any form of reprisals against us!

We were still facing the dilemma as to how we might be reunited with our brothers. Both Francis and I had very limited recollections of life at Charlton Park. This probably emphasises how important George and John were in filling in the voids in our collective memories of events at that time. I can remember feeling very disconnected with the other boys there and terribly homesick for our former lives together at Ashley Coombe. Over the years I had acquired the nickname Tubs, to reflect my healthy appetite and the fact that I was as tall as I was round. However, over the ensuing months our appetites dampened and my clothes began to feel too loose on me. Was I wasting away? After, what seemed ages, we had still not heard from our brothers. Our demeanour and well-being continued to decline and we no longer felt inclined to play out, to listen to the radio or to do anything.

Our general constitution must have come to the attention of Sir who one day gave us the news that we were yearning to hear. We were told that, since George and John were too old to come to Charlton Park, the decision had been made, that we should remain together as a family of brothers. As a result of this we were to be reunited with them again and soon. In spite of being under the official age for that home, we were, at last, leaving Charlton Park for Marfords. I remember feeling so overwhelmed and jubilant at the prospect of our reunion that I almost mistimed my visit to the bathroom to spend a penny.

Francis and I were both over the moon with the news and we decided that we couldn't wait any longer and returned to our dorm to start packing our belongings together. The fact that it was almost a week before we left didn't matter to us. It was just a waiting game now!

The wait soon came to an end when we were instructed to meet nurse under the hall clock at precisely ten o clock the next morning, but only after we had breakfast and had carried out our chores. Once the word had got out that we were leaving some of the other boys came to our dorm to say goodbye and/or commiserate with us that we were going to an unknown place.

One of the key lessons that I learned while I was in the care of Barnardo's was the importance of continuity and routine in our lives. This was very important for us lads. We needed to know that we would eat, play, sleep and wash at a particular time every day with no element of doubt that they might not take place. Our leaving Charlton Park was considered by the boys as a disrupter to this. They all said that they were happy that they were staying behind. Unusually for me I must have been feeling particularly kind and generous at the prospect of our forthcoming reunion. Never one for giving my prized possessions away and definitely not the type of person who shares anything of his own, I actually decided to leave my best conker and bonce marble to the young lad in the next bed to mine. The next day we were taken by a taxi to the station and then by train to Cheshire.

We hadn't much experience of meeting "outsiders" or of even being outside the homes. For us steam trains were only ever seen in books and so this outing was to be a real adventure for the two of us. After eating a sandwich that nurse had brought us for lunch, we both had forty winks and before we knew it we were at our destination.

Bromborough at last and the long awaited reunion.

It was dark when we arrived at the entrance to Marfords and so it was unclear to us exactly what it looked like. That would have to wait for another day. In the meantime we had supper and were then taken by nurse to our dorm. I have to say that I was disappointed that my brothers were not around to greet us. It had been months since we had last seen them and I thought that they would have been as excited to see me as I was to see them.

Discipline & strict timing, meeting
our brothers again and School.

I guess to say that we were disappointed at the sight that confronted us, as the door opened, would have been an understatement. The dorm was nothing like Ashley Coombe and as we entered it our faces fell. Although we never had many personal possessions our bed was our territory and we were always encouraged to make it look the way we wanted. In contrast, this place seemed to lack this and there was nothing at all to suggest that there were young lads in residence here. The room, itself, was very plain and ordinary and the walls were whitewashed, not painted in pastel colours. There were no pictures, no football team posters and, in fact, nothing to suggest that anything had ever been hung on them before. There were no shadow-creating side lights or standard lamps, just a bright centre light. However perhaps the strangest sight were the beds themselves. The bedding was all identical in colour and the beds had been made in a very specific and precise way with the top layers accurately folded into a pleat with the top sheet turned down a certain distance at the top. I wondered who it was that might make the "boys" beds to all look the same! It seemed to me to be very orderly and nothing like we had experienced before.

Although we never had much it seemed, from a first impression, that none of the boys had any personal belongings at all like we had at Ashley Coombe. The absence of any toys or comics/books on the table or on the floor was very worrying and Francis reckoned that they must have been "out of bounds" in the dorm!

It quickly became clear to us that the dorm was strictly for sleeping in and not for congregating in, playing in or for having any sort of fun at all.

What sort of a place was Marfords? Had we, in fact, been taken to a prison?

Looking around we noticed that the boys' clothes were neatly folded and placed in the same location on the top of the locker. It was if somebody had marked a precise area out for the children to place their individual bundles of clothing. None of the piles were out of place and each were secured with a snake belt, and one other thing, not one of the boys spoke to us, not even to ask who we were.

Upon our arrival they were already in bed. However, some of them peeked out from under their bedding. We introduced ourselves and told them that we had been on a long train journey and that we had come to Marfords to join our older brothers again. There were lots of "shushing and hushing" from the other beds and then one boy whispered to us "to be quiet as there was no talking after lights out".

Francis whispered to me "It's more like a military barracks than a dorm." Anyway we undressed for bed and spent our first night in Marfords a little disconcerted by the dorm but excited at the prospect of our forthcoming reunion with George and John.

I have to say that it wasn't long before we both began to wonder whether we had made the right choice in asking to be taken to this place at all. Things didn't seem to improve in the short term as our eventual reunion with George and John did not go quite as I had expected. I have to admit to being a bit of a drama queen and so I had certain expectations as to how our reunion might go. I anticipated that as we met our brothers again that they would suffer from an uncontrolled attack of sniffulitis, you know tears of joy at our reunion. This would then have been followed by comforting cuddles, just to reassure us that we had been missed, and that it was great to be back altogether again. In reality this could not have been further from the truth and nothing quite prepared us for their actual response to seeing us again!

The next morning Francis and I were the first to get up. We were both washed, dressed and ready for breakfast long before the other boys had even stirred. As we patiently waited by our beds for the others to come around from their deep sleep we heard a hideous crescendo of sound emanating from the lawn area in the front of the house. The sound was almost indescribable somewhere between a poor hen being throttled and a klaxon hooter at full blast. It was a sound that, thankfully, I had never heard before and I hope that I wouldn't hear again.

We both rushed to the window to see what the source of the commotion was. It was at that moment that we saw the view from our window for the first time and it was a very pleasant view indeed. In the front was a very large lawn and in the distance was woodland, reminding me of the woods at Porlock and of better times. As we both looked down onto the front of the lawn we saw a boy blowing furiously on what I later discovered was a bugle. His cheeks were ballooning out so far that we couldn't see either his eyes or his nose. He looked very odd indeed.

As we looked on in awe Francis reminded me that was how I looked when I held my breath to get my own way. I decided, there and then, that if I looked that hideous then I would never do it again. I was quite proud of my looks and I wouldn't want anyone to think that I was as ugly as bugle-boy in full blast.

"What the hell was that racket for?" said Francis to the boy in the next bed,

"It's Charlie, Charlie get out of bed. Our morning reveille, it's to wake us up, rise and shine. We wake to that every morning. Where the hell have you both come from"?

He went on tell us that everything is done to the bugle or the bells. The bugler tells us when it's mealtime with "Come to the cook-house door boys," and at bedtime with "Light's out and no talking".

"And the bells?" said Francis.

"Oh that's Aldwinkle (the new Sir). He was in the Navy and likes us to do things to the bells. You'll soon find out how it works," said the boy in the next bed.

I remember thinking that he was very rude to call Sir "old winkle" but just then the nurse came bursting in. She barked at us that we had eight minutes to wash, change for breakfast and be ready in-line by the door.

"I suppose that you two are the new boys. Well we do things differently here," she said.

As the boys assembled in-line by the dormitory door she grabbed hold of Francis and said "That's your place, Sonny Jim" and she then did the same to me.

She told us "that we must never forget our place in the line or there would be trouble, real big trouble".

At the appropriate time she opened the door of the dorm and we marched, en masse, to the dining room. As we marched along I asked Francis "who was Sonny Jim? Whether he was a new boy like me? Why was the nurse so bad tempered?"

He reckoned "that he didn't know anybody called Sonny Jim and that she probably calls all boys Sonny Jim".

"Well that's all very confusing" I replied, "How are we to know which Sonny Jim she was referring to".

"Tubs why don't you just shut up asking daft questions" said Francis

"Well here's another one for you, stop being beastly to me" then I said, "Why is she so bad tempered with us? After all we haven't been here long enough to have done anything wrong. It's all too unfair!"

Francis remarked "that he wasn't too sure but he knew that it was very, very private and that it was to do with women's things.

I asked him "What sort of things were women's things".

He said "You know, to do with things downstairs", pointing to his belt region, "and things like that"

Well I didn't really have a clue what he was referring to and asked him "whereabouts downstairs did he actually mean" to which he replied "The place, you know downstairs, where only women are allowed to go".

"Why are only women allowed to go down there" I said "That's

29

terribly unfair on us and anyway why would that make her so terribly bad tempered with us especially as we are not allowed to go downstairs with them!"

Francis replied, "For crying out loud Tubs just shut up for one minute will you. Your questions just goes on and on and on and on". At that moment nurse told us to stop talking immediately as it was not allowed. I was really, really confused with both women and life in this place!

As the door to the dining room was opened I saw my older brothers for the first time in months and immediately felt overcome with joy and emotion. To my surprise they remained somewhat lofty and aloof to us. They both just looked around at us and smiled. They then carried on talking with the other boys on their table. No tears, no snivels, no cuddles no reassuring hugs, no nothing!

We were both surprised at how tall they had become and John was almost unrecognisable as his face was thinner and his shoulders so much broader. I reached the opinion that that wasn't enough of a greeting for me and I wanted much more from them. I decided to make my own way over to them and take them to task at not becoming "overcome with emulsion" like I had expected them to be! I was stopped by the same nurse, you know the one with women's troubles downstairs, who told me to stay in line and to make my way to our table.

During breakfast I asked Francis, in a whisper, what he thought was wrong with them and why they hadn't come over to speak to us or to welcome us back. We soon found out why from the boy opposite us. He informed us that our brothers "were not to be messed with as one of them, I assumed to George, was a table monitor and that the biggest boy on the table, in this case John, kept everybody else in their place.

"See," said Francis, "that's why they are acting a bit stand-offish; they are overseers now".

In a way we both felt rather proud of them but I was still a bit urdy at being ignored. As I looked around the dining room it was clear that there was a pecking order in operation. The large boys, sitting at two tables, had priority and queued first for breakfast, followed by the medium boys who were next and finally the small boys who queued up last. Yes the pecking order was large, medium and small just like eggs. Breakfast was fairly typical, consisting of a dollop of gooey porridge splodged onto a plate, some bread and jam and a cup of tea. Technically talking was not permitted at the table during mealtimes but we could whisper, gesticulate and pull manic faces at each other. Fortunately for me I was a master at all three forms of communication of that kind. The masters and nurses, who were seated on the top table, could see all in front of them and they made sure that we were all being well behaved. As meals came to an end Sir would permit quiet talking but no raising the voice and no talking across the tables.

I asked the boy next to me "Which one of the masters was old winkle?"

He replied that he didn't eat with us. As an old sea-dog he preferred to eat in the officers' mess in his digs.

I remember thinking that this place was very confusing. The masters and boys not only refer to Sir by a very rude name, but, they actually call him this to his face. They also reckoned that Sir lived in a mess. We were made to do chores, to ensure that everything was "tickety-boo", and that we were punished if we failed to have clean hands and clean finger nails. Yet Sir could live in a mess if he chose to. It's not fair and it's double standards!

As breakfast came to an end nurse approached Francis and me to inform us that we were each responsible for washing up our own breakfast things in the kitchen and that one of the boys also had to wipe the table down. Finally once that was done we had to meet her again promptly at 9.00 a.m. in the hall to the sound of two bells.

After cleaning up our breakfast things we waited in the hall when, suddenly, John and George came by to meet us. We rushed up to them and flung our arms around them and told them how much we had missed them. They seemed a little cagey and nervous at our response and kept looking around the hall to see if any of their contemporaries were present and looking on. John then told us that things here in Marford's were little different, compared to Ashley Coombe. He told us that they might not be around all the time during the week as they both went to school locally. Also they had responsibilities, as older boys, which meant that we might have to share them more with the other boys. I was taken back by this: they were our brothers not anybody else's and it was unfair that we had to share. John looked down at us though, smiled and held our hands as only our big brother could, and said "Don't worry, we will still be here for you and yes, we are both very pleased to see you". We looked at each other again and they reckoned that although Francis was a bit bigger I was very much taller than they remembered me being. I asked them whether they were sleeping in the green-house because they had grown so much and that they were now both taller and wider than I remembered them. At that we said all that was needed to be said and I felt very reassured and safe again. Perhaps this place wouldn't be too bad after all.

Suddenly we were startled by the sound of two bells and John and George scurried off. We all took our place in the line as nurse approached. However, she asked Francis and me to wait behind in the hall while she took the others away for chores duty. She returned and told us that there was an important person for us to meet. We all went into an office and we asked nurse what it was all about. The door opened and a tall old man with white hair stood at the door and said "Attention". When we didn't respond the nurse whispered that we should have stood up from our chairs.

Again he said "Attention" and we both stood up, and he said, "Good. Now sit down both of you".

He said that he was Mr Aldwinkle and he was the Superintendent at Marford's. He said that he liked to run a tight ship and that meant listening for the bugle in the morning and evening and the ships bell for other important activities; that he knew about our particular circumstances, and that we needn't think that just because we were the youngest we would get our own way. He told us that as it was early September we would both be going "outside", of the home, to attend the local primary school at Bromborough Cross and starting on the following Monday. He hoped that we would soon settle in and adapt to life at Marford's and we would learn both, from the other boys and from our brothers, what acceptable behaviour was and what was not. That was all.

Over the coming days Francis and I decided that, as new boys, it was best to just go with the flow, to try to agree with everyone, do what we were told without question and try not to create waves, and definitely not to anger Old Winkle!

That day one of the nurses bought Francis and I a special "outsider" outfit to wear for school. It was a memorable occasion because the trousers were made of very itchy material. Francis made the comment that I mustn't keep scratching myself "down there" as the other boys might think that I was a pansy or something like that. Although I was desperate I decided not ask the obvious question about what a flower had to do with me. Instead I remained like Dad and kept Mum. To be honest I wasn't really too sure what that expression meant either. I was just very confused all of the time. Also, on that same day, we had our photographs taken (right).

This picture is me (above) taken on my first day at school

Me and Francis on our first day at school

We were told that the photographs were to go into our files. I didn't really understand what he meant by that; and to be completely honest with you I didn't really care I was just looking forward to seeing what it was like on the "outside". That was going to be a new experience for us both.

Monday morning, and my first day at school, soon came around and, in some respects, I was quite excited at the prospect. As well as having to be ready for an extra early breakfast Francis and I had to do our chores and then change into our "outsider" clothes for school. Having changed we assembled on the front lawn for daily kit inspection just as the ship's bell rang. All the boys had formed their respective lines on the lawn and it was then that I saw George and John in their long school trousers. The last time we were together at Ashley Coombe they had worn short trousers, like me.

A whistle blew and Sir came out of the door and walked along the line of big boys. It was like some sort of military inspection parade however neither of us were sure what to expect or what he was actually looking for. I guess that Francis and I had not been given the whole drill! Fortunately, for us, he started his morning inspection with the other older boys first and it followed the same drill. As the master stopped by each boy they would offer him their hands to ensure that they were clean, their shoes, to ensure that they were polished and then, strange as it may sound, the linings of their pockets. I whispered, out of the corner of my mouth to the next boy, "why their pocket linings?"

"Because they didn't have a clean hanky on them," he whispered back, "If we forget our hanky we just show the linings of our pockets instead."

"Blimey," I said to Francis "This is like the army and we haven't got a hanky. We'll have to show our pocket lining too".

As Old Winkle approached me I was shaking with fear, my shoes were scuffed and I was scared about the hanky business. I thought that I was in for it. Actually, it all went well and when the whistle blew again, to mark the end of the parade, our respective nurses emerged came to accompany us, in our marching lines, to Bromborough Cross (the Cross) where the primary and secondary schools were located. Francis and I were officially registered to attend Bromborough Cross infant's school and John and George at the junior school, just across the road from our school. I was taken into my class by a Barnardo nurse and left there on my own and Francis went to another class with the Medium Eggs (the medium boys).

I remember that I began to feel very uncomfortable on my own and

I have to confess that I hated the experience so much that I immediately started to scream out that I wanted my brothers. I then resorted to sitting down on the floor and kicking my feet up and down as I hollered on the top of my voice. I did tell you that I was a bit of a drama queen!

Looking back at the situation I believe that the teacher dealt with it with great sympathy and compassion considering that I was a new boy and that I was on my own - I don't think so! She made me stand in the corner, behind the blackboard, with my back to the class as an example to other boys in the class. That, however, didn't work and I still acted up before graduating to tears and loud "snotty" sobbing. In time they got the message and brought Francis into me. The two of us were then taken across the road to the Junior School where we sat playing with wooden bricks until John and George came out. I think I kept up the tantrums for a few days before eventually settling down to school life.

What an introduction!

It is my belief that my early experiences of school life in Bromborough, in those first few days of my formal education, actually shaped my attitude and approach to learning from then on. I am not suggesting that the teaching was in any way poor; on the contrary, I have very happy memories of the school life, once I had settled in. Basically, I liked the school and because I was quite tall for my age I somehow attracted respect from my peers in the class, and for me that was a good thing as I never had any cheek from any of them. Also I thrived on the discipline of school life and in that way I was considered to be a model pupil.

However, it was the process of assimilating knowledge, learning all the facts and figures, reciting our tables, identifying who said what and why? It just did my head in. My mind was too crammed full of other stuff to undertake yet another task with any sort of commitment. I loved listening to music and poetry but during the actual lessons themselves I was away with the fairies. Most of the time I would just look out of the window admiring the beauty and wondering about my brothers or what we might have for supper that night or how was Teddy? How could I possibly assimilate any more data when my brain already seemed to be filled up to capacity? I was one of life's daydreamer; an activity that did not pass unnoticed by the teachers. It is true to say that on most of my school records, from then on, I was highly commended for my obedience, politeness and articulacy but with the caveat - William needs to spend less time daydreaming and try harder to concentrate in class!

It was not all marching, standing to attention and doing things to the whistle and/or ship's bell in the home, and once a week we would have a treat. The nurse would walk with the boys into the Cross and take us to the sweet shop.

Although I wasn't too sure what being on-ration actually meant I definitely knew that the consequences meant that I couldn't have as many sweets as I wanted. In the early 1950's we were only limited to four ounces per person per week. As this was my first official trip to the sweet shop I had already been advised, by a more experienced boy, to only select the smaller sweets because that way you got more for your money!

It was very intriguing just how accomplished the shopkeeper was at making little cones, out of brown squares of paper, ready to add our selection. When it came to my turn I was already profusely salivating. I was beside myself at the joyous sight of rows upon rows of sweeties of every shape and size imaginable.

Slurpingly I said "I'll have four of those", pointing to sherbert lemons, "and two of those" (sherbert UFOs) "four of those" (fruit salad drops), "four of those" (blackjacks) and "two of those" (gob stoppers).

"That's your lot Sonny. What can I take out. You've got too many?" said the shopkeeper.

I was astonished on two accounts. Just how did he know that my selection was over four ounces and secondly was he a friend of the nurse, back at Marfords, because she also referred to me as Sonny.

"Actually, Sir, my name's William not Sonny" I said to him.

He told me "to stop buggering about with him or he'd give me a thick ear. I haven't got the time to mess around with you. Just give me back a gob stopper and we will be quits". That was duly done!

What I did not anticipate was that back in the dorm there would immediately be a communal swap-shop. For various reasons I decided that on this occasion I would keep all of my sweets for myself as I wanted to try them and savour them all, by myself, for the first time. I didn't realise however, the need for me to guard them or to hide them in a secret place. Only when I returned from supper and the "lights out bugle" had sounded I went to my cache for a midnight feast and found half of them had been taken. I looked around the dorm at the other boys but none were looking any guiltier than they did usually and although I asked the perpetrator to own up but, alas for me, nobody did.

Lesson learned; and I made sure that it would never happen again. Over time I grew accustomed to the ruses and pranks that went on at Marfords and I remember thinking that so long as none was ever successfully carried out upon me I would be happy. From that day on none was and I was happy about that. It meant that I could sleep better at night.

The Festival of Britain, Alvar Lidell, a missing child and a fire in the den.

It was in 1951, about the time that Francis and I were due to leave Charlton Park, that wireless broadcasters spoke relentlessly about the Festival of Britain that was scheduled to take place in London in that year. Being the youngest boys living in the "Marford's" all of the excitement that this generated was lost on us as we were more or less in the dark as to what was going on in the outside world. To us the festival was of no great significance but for the older boys it took on a whole new meaning.

Unlike Ashley Coombe, here, the older boys had their own common room, complete with a wireless, so every evening they could sit around it and listen to the current developments going on the world. The one event that really captured their imagination was the Festival of Britain. I distinctly remember John telling us that it was an exhibition about the future of Britain and space exploration. He became very keen on the Festival and, although he was unable to visit London at the time, he was still infatuated with its premise. John's eyes would glaze over as he told us about the Futurama Exhibition.

This included the Dome of Discovery and a rocket shaped structure called the Skylon (above) and if that wasn't enough excitement there was a futuristic funfair.

I guess you could say that there was something for everybody.

About that time John became very cagey and secretive about what he was getting up to. In the evening, when he said he was going to his common room, George inadvertently let the cat out of the bag and told us that John wasn't actually with him. I knew he was up to something. But what exactly?

When I asked him directly, where he was, he just said something along the line that I needed to keep my gob shut and that all would be revealed shortly, or maybe he said shorty instead! He told me that if I kept on about it I would spoil the fun for all the other boys but it had something to do with the Festival of Britain.

I didn't like it when I was being kept "in the dark" over something and just as I was about to start to hold my breath again John said "and if you try the breath-holding trick Tubs, I'll give you a good slapping on your mush". I thought it best to retreat over and talk to George instead.

Francis and I were beside ourselves with excitement, not only because we knew a secret that nobody else knew but that John was involved in something that was going to thrill and entertain us. Despite reminding some of the lads that I was the holder of a big secret and that nobody would ever be able to get the secret out of me

I did actually manage to keep mum.

The following weekend the news was circulated that at four bells all of we boys must meet together at the bottom end of the slope in the front garden. To say that the boys were beside themselves with excitement would not be an exaggeration. As we waited expectantly, I was holding Francis's hand, when we suddenly heard a terrible rhythmic metallic clattering noise coming from the top of the hill. Dispersed between the metallic clattering was a thwacking sound. It was a real crescendo of noises and the gardeners came running out to see what all of the commotion was about.

Suddenly there he was, our brother John, riding what looked like a bike but that sounded like nuts and bolts being shaken up in a tobacco tin. He was being chased by George. The thwacking noise was a wooden strip that clicked through the spokes of the wheels as they rotated. It was a joy to see. His long skinny legs were all akimbo and he shouted for us to keep the path clear because he had no brakes and no tyres. As he came closer we could see that his bike had a big sign on the front which read "The Festival of Britain bike 1951".

Stopping the bike was another matter and demanded true grit as once it started to roll downhill you just had to go with it until it came to a standstill naturally.

The excitement among the boys was palpable and everybody wanted a go on his bike. In fact it was far too dangerous for the younger boys to ride by themselves. For a start John couldn't lift the wheels up because they were only kept in place by a promise and a six inch nail and the handlebar and saddle wobbled all over place. To be fair, nobody really cared about health and safety; in those days and the bike was made for us all to share on this magical occasion. John told us that the small boys could have a go provided either he or George steered it and stood behind them on specially made treads that they had installed when they made it. Yes, it would be true to say that the Festival of Britain bicycle had been the highlight of the summer and one of the biggest talking points of that year. There was, I am happy to report, much, much more excitement to follow. John was now on a rollercoaster of inventiveness with ideas a plenty to entertain the boys.

Shortly after the Festival bike he went into another secretive phase and I knew he was up to something, yet, again. He knew that we youngsters were not allowed into their common room and so none of the Small Eggs had much of an idea about just what a wireless did or what a wireless was capable of doing. Journey into space were just three words to us, we knew nothing about the exciting goings-on, and so John decided that he wanted to do something about that! So for his next show-stopping venture he decided to do something about this disparity.

This time he came up with an ingenious way to illustrate to us the entertainment value of the wireless. Over the next few days he and George spent all of their spare time carrying out the necessary preparation to give the boys another treat. Being naturally very nosy I secretly followed them and saw George digging a hole in the lower garden area. At that time George seemed to be spending a lot of his time digging holes and I came to the conclusion that this was what he had in mind as a future career. I quite admired his enthusiasm at such an early stage. However, once again I had it all wrong. After breakfast one morning we Small and Medium Eggs were told to remain behind while the older boys left. Once we were on our own John got up from his table and announced to us that there was to be a special wireless transmission for us all in the lower garden precisely at six bells. The boys became very excited and rushed off to their chores in good time.

When we arrived at the meeting place in the garden we were greeted by what looked like an old wireless. We didn't know this immediately but John was actually sitting inside the wireless. His legs were in the hole in the ground that George was digging when I was spying on them.

In fact we later discovered that he and George had actually made the wireless out of cardboard boxes. We all sat there, in the round, looking at the dial of the wireless and waiting, in anticipation, for something to happen. Believe me you could hear a pin drop.

All of a sudden a light came on from the lower left hand side of the dial, presumably from a torch, at the same time as George turned the radio on with a control on the lower right. He then announced that he was going to tune the radio into the correct wavelength for us to hear the News of the Day. At that George turned the knob around and began to make twangy, squeaky noises as he tuned it in. Suddenly to our astonishment we heard a voice saying,

"Good Morning, this is the Home Service and this is your news reader Alvar Lidell."

Well we just sat there mesmerised and looking intently at the wireless with our mouths ajar, waiting with bated breath to hear the headlines. The newsreader then asked us if we were sitting comfortably.

None of us knew whether to respond or not and so Alvar asked us again "Are you sitting comfortably?" We replied "Yes," to which he said "I cannot hear you boys. Speak louder," and we all cried out "Yes" at the tops of our voices. I thought to myself what fun this was.

"*Here is the news on the Home Front,*" said Alvar.

"Buckingham Palace was thrown into darkness today when the Queen dropped her shilling for the electric meter. She was later quoted as saying that it took her maid twenty minutes to find it after it rolled under the corgi's bed.

News just in: Prince Philip has been made an Honorary Major of the 1st. Highland Foot and Mouth Regiment.

Buckingham Palace have denied rumours that when Prince Philip visited a Scottish Driving Instructor Convention in Edinburgh he enquired, "How do you keep the natives off the booze long enough to pass the test?"

"*Here is news from the Empire*".

The winner of the Empire pie-eating competition is a Mr Ram Jam Full.

A Mr. Mustapha Phag recently came first in the International smoking competition.

The winner of the East Asian muck spreading competition was Mr. Who Flung Dung.

Finally, the first woman to lose her job in a telephone exchange was a Miss Wing Wong. A spokesman for the company told reporters that she just couldn't get the numbers right and kept winging the wong number.

"Well boys that is all the News from me here at the Home Service," said Alvar Lidell. "Next time", he said, "make sure that you tune in for Dick Barton-special agent and follow the adventures of Captain Dick Barton and his mates Jock and Snowy as they solve crimes, escape from dangerous situations, and save the country from ruin. So all I have to say to you now is Goodbye children where ever you are but especially those of you in the Small Eggs dorm".

At that the light went out on the wireless and we got up to leave. However it came back on again and, with it, came Alvar who repeated his last message to us: "Goodbye children wherever you are".

We all turned back towards the wireless and waved goodbye and shouted "Goodbye Alvar".

One of the traditional Sunday afternoon entertainments was for the children to be accompanied by a master for long walks in the surrounding countryside and, as Francis and I were now older, it was decided that we could join them. I was hoping that John and George might be with us too but they said that they would prefer to stay back and hang out with their friends in the scout hut. I sort of understood what they meant but nevertheless, was disappointed in them. Francis and I had some making up to do and so we walked double pace to catch the other boys up. It was raining and so we wore our school caps and Wellington boots on the walk. The area that we visited was called Raby Mere, part of Dibbinsdale, a local nature reserve, parkland and ancient woodland and, fortunately for us we could walk to it from Marfords.

I guess that the master was in a good mood on this occasion because he first took us to parklands to play on the swings and slides and then, later, into the woods. We loved the play area at Raby Mere, especially the swings and the boat swings, and would scream our heads off in excitement. For us the boat swing was a pirate ship and we were all on the look-out for booty and walking around saying "Aaaah Jim lad". Our main game, however, was called the parachute jump which involved seeing which of the boys could swing the highest before ejecting themselves from the swing, in mid-air, and then landing upright on their feet. The important point for the boys was that you had to land upright and if you fell, as you landed, you would be grounded until the next visit to the park. One of the other lads oversaw that this important decision was enforced.

To be quite honest I hated it as I was basically frightened and the thought of all that movement, to and fro, made me feel that I would lose my lunch. I thought it best that I remain with my feet firmly on the ground. This was a favourite game of the boys. However, this particular master had clearly never seen us perform it before. He blew his whistle and, to our absolute horror, forbad us from doing it again.

We thought he was a bit of a spoilsport and a rotter especially when he told us not to descend the slide backwards or on our tummies and that we were forbidden to jump off directly from the top of the slide or to attempt to reach the top of the slide by scaling up the metal framework instead of climbing the steps. A game we called climbing Everest.

Overall, I guess that he had his work cut out keeping his eyes on this boisterous bunch, but we still enjoyed every minute of freedom away from chores and bells. Moreover, and much to the master's surprise, we were quite a tough bunch and made it back to base with very few cuts or bruises.

As the rain was so persistent the master suggested that we should go for a walk in the woods instead. As we entered the woods it was soon clear that it was not such a good idea either, as it was dark and gloomy, and the path was extremely slippery and muddy underfoot. It didn't take the master long to realise that we were all going to become soaked to the skin so, in the interests of us all, he decided that we should forgo the walk and instead head back for an early afternoon tea. I was all for that, an early tea and all. As we left the wooded area and reassembled into our groups on the path the master suddenly noticed that Carter, one of the boys in our dorm, was wearing only one Wellington boot.

He asked Carter "what had happened to his other boot" and was told "that it had become stuck in the mud back in the woods and that he couldn't get it out again".

Carter was told that his boots cost a lot of money and that it was his responsibility to look after his kit. He then told him "to go back in and retrieve it while we waited for him". Even though we were only young children we were all surprised that the master had made the decision to send Carter in on his own.

Francis reckoned "that we should all have gone to help Carter to find his boot as he might be in grave danger on his own at night".

We had all heard about the things that come to life in the woods as the light begins to fail. We were becoming worried about Carter and that he might be spending the night in the woods all by himself!

We seemed to have been waiting for ages and as the light began to fade it was decided that we should head back to Marfords without Carter. It was my guess that this would also mean that we would not be having our afternoon tea either! On our arrival back some of the bigger boys went with the masters to resume the search for Carter. We later heard that they had no luck and that the local police had become involved.

As far as we all knew nothing like this had ever happened before and back in the dorm there was much speculation as to the fate of Carter. The fat boy, Johnson, told us that he had heard stories about the travelling country folk that lived in those woods and the goings-on that took place. We were now very intrigued by Johnson. In fact to be perfectly honest with you I had never heard him speak before, only whisper, and I was surprised at how well he spoke and that he had an opinion and was even able to express himself. In fact I was surprised that he had any thoughts of his own about anything!

"Apparently", said Johnson, "they like to do things their way and they don't like anybody poking their noses into their business".

As we all sat around my bed he continued, "At certain times of the year, especially when it has been raining heavily or there is a waxing moon, they are sometimes unable to find their favourite snack food in the form of hedgehogs. Then they become very prickly and agitated and their hunger makes them very, very urdy and then they are liable to change and eat something or somebody else. You wouldn't want to mess with these folk when they are like that I can tell you".

"What", I said "Do they actually eat hedgehogs? That's disgusting".

"Shut up Tyrrell and let me finish," said Johnson. "Yes, when it's too wet outside the hedgehogs have to run to dry land for safety, and it is then, that these folk have to look for other kinds of flesh to eat".

One of the other boys then made the observation that Carter had plenty of flesh on his body. "Yes," said Johnson, "if they find Carter that might well be his fate. Even now, as we speak, Carter could be in the pot ready to be eaten for tea."

"Oh poor Carter," said Francis.

As well as the possibility that Carter was, at that precise moment, bring consumed by a group of cannibals, another of our group, Edgington, threw in an alternative fate for Carter. Although I had heard about this phenomenon I had never personally witnessed it for myself. Thank God! Edgington, on the other hand, was convinced about it and said that it helped to explain why so many people just mysteriously disappeared into thin air.

He told us "that when one was "outside" one should never get too close to a cow. Also, and even more importantly, never, ever approach the rear of a cow. Doing such a thing invokes an immediate involuntary reaction from Daisy-Belle. As you approach a cow from behind it causes it to suck-up through their backside and, if you or anyone else happens to be within sucking distance, they will almost certainly be sucked up as well."

"That," we were told, "was a fate worse than death".

It wasn't too long before this nonsense was also brought to the table with the suggestion that it might explain the fate of Carter; that in the dark of the night Carter had approached too close to a cow and been sucked up its backside.

Two of the boys reckoned that it was a true and a well-known fact and that they personally knew someone who knew somebody else who had a friend who had died in that way. They added that after consuming someone, in that particular way, their bones were violently ejected back out again through the same orifice.

"What's an orifice" I asked?

"Shut up Tyrrell let them continue" the other boys retorted.

They also suggested that on occasions whole intact and clothed skeletons had been blasted out from the cow's backside. I guess that on a positive note this made identification of the deceased much easier.

Francis was very sceptical and said to us "that this sounded like a load of old baloney". However, there was caveat to his scepticism I hasten to say. Francis did actually ask one of the older boys, involved in the search, whether they had found a pile of bones in the woods or a fully clothed skeleton with only one Wellington boot on. He gave a great sigh of relief when he said they had not.

That night we all went to bed punctually with lots on our mind; I laid in bed still slightly miffed that our afternoon tea had been so over-shadowed by the events of a Wellington boot. The next morning we were woken, extra early, by the bugler, who was playing an unfamiliar tune that sounded like a chicken being throttled. The boy in the next bed told us that it was probably a fire drill and that we needed to assemble, just as we were, immediately. In fact we were the last to assemble in front of the main door and as Old Winkle came out we all stood to attention.

"Stand at ease boys," he said. He went on to tell us that this was not an official fire drill but that he wanted to update us about Carter. "Carter is safely back home and resting in the sick bay," he told us. He then informed us that Carter had, in fact, been found by the police at the traveller's camp and that he had been well cared for by them. According to their leader they had been alerted by his screaming and yelling out in the darkness. He reckoned that the racket Carter was making was so loud that he could have been heard from the Liver Building.

Actually, that was not the end of the story.

Although I don't think formally it went any further, some rather serious allegations were made by Carter about his treatment at Marfords and that he wanted to remain with the people that saved him. Sending a young boy back into the woods on his own at dusk does not suggest that a very caring and considerate decision had been reached. A story began to circulate, although in no way substantiated, that the spokesperson for the travellers was at first reluctant to cooperate with the police. He told them that Carter had made claims of ill-treatment at Marfords and that he would prefer to remain with them in Raby Mere and Dibbensdale Woods. In truth, they didn't have any obligation to Carter and eventually handed him back.

Back in the dorm we had a short, pre-breakfast pow-wow to discuss what we could do for Carter once he had gotten over his shock and was safely back with us. We decided upon two options the first was specifically to help Carter and the second was to specifically help us just in case we found ourselves in a similar situation to Carter.

So each of us decided to donate some of our sweets to Carter. Secondly, we would ask him whether he actually found his boot in the woods or not. If he hadn't found it then just how did he intend to avoid the wrath of Sir for carelessly losing it in the first place? It might seem rather mean gaining an advantage over somebody else's misfortune but a similar event might easily happen to one of us in the future. A possible solution to the problem would be jolly helpful for us.

Over the coming weekends I definitely sensed that John and George were up to no good again. When we did ask them how things were going they remained tight lipped, and from this Francis and I assumed that they had other more important, but secret, schemes going on. It shouldn't really have been much of a surprise to us that the older boys preferred to keep mum about their projects. After all they mainly did what they did for our entertainment and the possibility that a snitch, even their little brother, might have spoiled things for them.

Actually it became a bit of a custom for us to make our own entertainment because, at Marfords, we had very few, if any, toys or comics and so the Little Eggs were definitely reliant upon the Large Eggs for diversions and fun. Well, George really excelled himself this time.

I mentioned, earlier, that George had a penchant for digging holes. Well, to be absolutely honest with you if you gave him a shovel and a plot of grass a hole would appear before you could say, "Mole, what Mole?" Well on this particular occasion his enthusiasm got the better of him as unbeknown to us he had actually dug an underground den with room for him and his mates to sit in. What's more, for extra security and privacy, George decided to dig it out way beyond the "Out of bounds to boys" signs that punctuated our outdoor play areas. If a boy crossed over any one of those signs and was caught by a master he would certainly have been in deep trouble. I had never met an offender but one of the large eggs said that you would be made to walk the plank, by Old Winkle, if you were caught. Nobody ever did!

We later discovered that the older boys had been using the den for some time for pow-wows or for just for hanging out together. In fact none of us younger boys had any knowledge about it until that fateful Sunday afternoon before tea. It seems that George had lined his den with old sacks and illuminated the interior with candles. Now I don't know whether this was a true story or not but John reckoned they as they had no access to matches they would light a candle using a hand lens to concentrate sunlight onto the wick. Anyway on this particular Sunday afternoon we nippers were playing by the path when one of them pointed towards a plume of smoke coming out of the ground.

We were frozen to the spot as we were not allowed to cross the "Out of Bounds" sign and so we waited, where we were, to see might happen. Within minutes we heard a spluttering and coughing noise coming from the direction of the smoke and from out of a hole in the ground came George and his mates. Apparently a lighted candle had fallen over and caught the sacking alight. George told us that he was so busy talking with his friends that none of them noticed anything untoward until they were coughing and choking. Although we never heard the outcome from this, or whether the boys were disciplined, as far as we knew George never dug another den. That really was a very close shave.

A new "Sir", a grumpy nurse, a theft, the chicken incident & Trial by Jury

Francis and I had been at Marfords for about a year when a notice appeared on the noticeboard, outside the playroom, to say that Mr. Aldwinkle was soon to retire. His replacement, Mr. Fuller, would then be taking over as the new Superintendent.

It was odd but I had never seen his name actually written down and was therefore very surprised to see the correct spelling. Throughout my time at Marfords I was under the naïve impression that people were being disrespectful in calling him Old Winkle and I was quite shocked at this realisation. It taught me a great lesson about making false assumptions but I still liked my interpretation of his name. Mine was much more fun – tee hee hee.

On the whole we small eggs had very little contact with him and so I wasn't too sure whether I would miss him or not. I certainly felt no sense of attachment to him and, in fact, I am not too sure whether he ever really made a lot of effort to really get to know the boys. Perhaps that was the best policy for a Superintendent, no attachments – no disappointments!

On his final Sunday afternoon Mr. and Mrs. Aldwinkle invited all of the boys to afternoon tea and said that we had to dress smartly. None of us thought that Mr. Aldwinkle was even married as we had never seen another woman in the home other than matron and the nurses and we were all very keen to see what she looked like!

In the afternoon we were marched into the dining room to the sound of the whistle with Sir standing to attention. The tea was really scrummy with lots of cakes and sandwiches. In fact there were so much to eat that some of us stored the leftovers into our pockets for later consumption. Towards the end of teatime one of the masters stood up and said a few words about how wonderful Mr Aldwinkle had been as a Superintendent, how much they and the boys would miss him and that it would be hard for his successor to match up to him. As a going away gift the masters presented Mrs Aldwinkle with flowers and Sir with a picture of the home and a book about the history of Bromborough.

I was surprised that Mrs Aldwinkle seemed to be genuinely upset at the situation as she kept wiping her eyes and blowing her nose. I said as much to Francis who replied that "She was either suffering from hay fever or she was crying with joy at the thought of leaving this old dump. Anyway there was nothing for her to miss because nobody knew she existed". That was the last that we saw of them and the next day, when we returned from school, the new Superintendent had already moved into his new digs.

Just before lights out, the following evening, we were all sitting on our beds in the dorm speculating about the changes that Mr Fuller might introduce and whether we would all be better off or not as a result. We began to list the changes that we would like to see including removing the out-of-bounds signs in the gardens, some comics to read, more sweets, not having to do things to the bell and also not having to stand to attention, which we thought was too much like the military. Actually, most of us wanted to be soldiers but we all disliked doing things to the bell! Perhaps our greatest wish was that the dreaded nurse Nasty would not reappear again. To us nippers she seemed to be an unfriendly nurse with little understanding of our needs. Fortunately, for us, she hadn't been around for a while and was certainly not being missed. One bright spark reckoned that she had been too close to the back of a cow however because she was so nasty she was instantly rejected and blown out again intact.

That, unfortunately, were our thoughts and regards about nurse Nasty!

It was Francis who was the unfortunate recipient of her harsh treatment when he first encountered her wrath in his very early days at Marfords. He told us of how, when he first arrived, the uncertainty of it all caused him to wet the bed. When she discovered this nurse

Nasty got very angry, almost taking his misdemeanour personally. She grabbed Francis, took him to the bathroom and told him to sit in a bath of cold water and think carefully about whether he thought it was kind to soil his sheets in that way. I was shocked by this, as Francis hadn't let on to me about it, and that he had to endure at least a further three cold ducking's before it stopped. In time, and no thanks to her, he gradually settled in and became more relaxed.

We were all nattering away and consoling Francis when the door of the dormitory suddenly flew open. There was instant silence, even quaking on the spot, for it was none other than nurse Nasty herself. One bright spark whispered that it was a full moon and another that the undead stalk the earth when the Sun went down and that we should all watch out for our necks and not to look her directly in her "eye"! Anyway we all wondered what this apparition of terror was doing back again perhaps she had returned to torment the living daylights out of us.

"Hello boys," she said, "it's good to be back. I am sure that I do not need to remind you, you all know the drill. Not one of you little scroungers pays a penny towards the electric so it's lights out and no talking".

At that she turned out the light and threw the dorm into complete darkness in her final unkind act of the day.

Actually, this wasn't her final act of the day at all.

Looking back at the situation I am unable to explain why I opened my mouth at the precise time that I did. How I wished that I had heeded the advice of my brothers about my need to moderate my articulating mandible. I deserved all that was to follow because of my sheer stupidity. I should have realised that if you are going to bad mouth somebody it is always a good idea to ensure that they are out of earshot and that they were no longer in the room. My one fundamental mistake occurred as nurse Nasty approached the door of the dorm. Unfortunately for me she was still in our presence in the darkened room when I called out, "bloody nurse Nasty, bloody nurse Nasty".

At that the light came on again and we could all see her in her incandescent "beauty", complete with flailing nostrils with her head pitched back as she began to bay to the moon. At that moment I knew that I was in big, big trouble. Suddenly a gnarled, smouldering talon appeared from nowhere and bodily hauled me up into the air. I was dragged from the safety of my dormitory into the bathroom whereupon this ghastly apparition of sheer horror pulled my head back and forced a bar of carbolic soap into my mouth.

I was crying with fear as the other boys screamed at her to desist. At the end she told me never to talk like that about her again or there would be real trouble. Her final words to us were, "If I hear any more from you lot I'll be back".

As she left the boys rallied around me, consoled me and gave me glasses of water to drink. To this day I have never really ever acquired a taste for carbolic soap in my mouth! That was a lesson that I would never forget, though upon reflection the experience was useful because she generously gave me some really useful tips on how I might handle myself when I was older and wiser.

John, in the meantime, reckoned that I probably deserved what I got as he believed that I needed to watch my tongue and that I was a gobby little so and so. Having said that, and realising that I was becoming distressed yet again by his attitude towards me, he followed it up with this caveat. He told me that he thought her individual actions were deplorable and totally unacceptable for somebody in the caring profession. He told me that whilst the Large Eggs felt inclined to complain about her bullying they nevertheless thought that it might inflame the situation as technically we were in the wrong. Swearing was not accepted in the homes and perpetrators were usually punished. In the end I was just very pleased for John's support.

The experience and trauma of this incident were insignificant compared to the excitement that followed shortly afterwards when Marfords had an unannounced visit from some unwelcome callers. It was the night when a dastardly crime was committed!

I was lying in bed recalling recent events, such as Carter and the travellers and the soap incident, which were playing heavily on my mind. I was so troubled that I actually turned to Francis and asked if I could bunk in with him for a while. I soon fell off to sleep.

At some time in the early morning Francis, who was always a very light sleeper, woke me up to tell me that he could hear some "activity" outside in the yard. "You're right," I agreed "It sounds like someone shovelling something up from the yard. Let's go and investigate". We decided to wake some of the other lads up, just for backing, and we all looked out of our dormitory window to see someone shovelling our coal from the coal bunker into the back of a van.

"Everest" said Francis, "go and get one of the masters pronto". We decided, as we didn't have a rope to climb down from the window, we would tie our pyjama cords together and then lasso the culprit just like Hopalong Cassidy did in the films. We were very excited at the prospect of catching the man out as he carried out his dastardly deed upon a children's home. As the master came into the dorm, along with Everest, we beckoned him to the window and informed him of our plan. At this stage most of us were having to hold our pyjama trousers up as Francis had already tied the cords into a very long lasso.

He was standing there spinning it around in the air and trying to hitch it, unsuccessfully, onto the bedposts. The main problem was that not only did it look nothing like a lasso but, as hard as we tried, we couldn't make it function as Hopalong did. It seemed that our efforts had been thwarted and now we had to rethread the cord back into our jimjams. Anyway it seemed that we had wasted our time because the master said that he was going to telephone the Police. He went on to tell us that under no circumstances were we to open the window or to alert the man to the fact that we had discovered him in action.

Actually he was already too late as one of the boys opened the window and blew his whistle so loud that we could hear the man shout out to himself "Come on our kid, you've been rumbled," and at that he made his get-a-way, complete with our coal.

Back in the dorm we were all too excited to go straight back to sleep and kept guessing how it might have been if we had been able to lasso the "dusky varmint".

One bright spark suggested "that it was very unlikely that PC Plod would ever recover our coal as the trail had now gone cold. You could say that he had been well and truly scuttled".

Always game for a challenge Francis suggested "that if the police failed to catch the culprit then they should be hauled over the coals by their bosses".

As this frivolity was taking place I took Everest to one side to enquire about a visitor that I had recently seen him with. I enquired about the dark lady who had been visiting him on a fairly regular basis over the past month or two. My main interest here lay in the large bag of sweets that she always left him and how I might get my hands on some of them as well.

"Well Tyrrell", said Everest, to be absolutely honest with you I have no idea why she picks on me to give sweets to and nobody else. She is very nice but she isn't a relative or anything. Sometimes after she has gone I feel frightened in case I get beaten up or something because of her favouritism. Do you think it is because I am like her?"

"Oh don't worry", I said greedily "we'll protect you if anyone picks on you. You have nothing to worry about as we all like you. Actually, I reckon that you would definitely improve your popularity if you decided that you wanted to share your sweets with us. As far as you both being similar, I am not sure what you mean!"

"Tyrrell", Everest said to me, "don't you think it's funny that she only visits me and gives me sweets and none of the others." Why do you think that is"?

I replied "She probably knew you in Africa. That must be the reason because I have never been to Africa and she doesn't know me or even come to see me with sweets or nothing! That's your reason".

He paused for a moment and then said "Tyrrell, where is Africa and why are the people different?"

"Blimey Everest I'm not really too sure but I think that Africa is definitely south of London and it's a long way away. Anyway people down there are different just like they are up here. Up here the people speak differently to those in the south and they call everybody our kid. So you see you are not that different after all."

"There is just one thing though, Tyrrell", replied Everest, "I don't think I have ever been to Africa. I have only ever been here although the lady said something about me coming from a place called Ackknee in East London."

I was now becoming a little lost for words with my explanations and so as a final assault I said "Well south or east of London it's still where Africa is. Perhaps when we go to school we can ask the master. We had better get some shut eye now Everest. Night Night, don't let the bed bugs bite, Oh and don't forget to say your prayers-we don't want to upset Jesus as well".

Life at Marfords continued pretty well unchanged even with the new Superintendent. He made some minor changes such as removing the "Out of Bounds" signage from the gardens and he stopping everything being done "to the bell". The bugle remained but one other change was that Mr Fuller now kept chickens on the lawn.

It was the responsibility of the Large Eggs to supervise the feeding of the chickens. A task they undertook with great professionalism apart from Craggy. He was a nasty piece of work, disliked by the Large and Medium Eggs alike. He was considered to be violent and very disruptive. We little ones were really shocked when his name appeared on the rota for feeding the chickens and cleaning out the coop. We could not, however, have foreseen what was to occur and the consequences of his actions.

On that particular occasion Craggy was attempting to round the chickens up either to feed them or to allow them into their coop for the night. One of the chickens made a "go for it" and instead of waiting or chasing it back Craggy decided to throw a big lump of wood at the bird.

The commotion the bird was making could be heard throughout the house and then suddenly there was silence! We rushed to the lawn to see Craggy pick the bird up and throw it into the bushes. We were all heartbroken and very upset by his callous treatment. In fact when Everest went to retrieve the carcass, for burial, he told us that Craggy had decapitated the poor bird and that he was laughing because the bird continued to run around in circles. Craggy also claimed that the bird had called out for his head to be put back on. I wasn't sure how much of that to believe. We were all livid and went to the older boys to snitch on the "fowl" deed that Craggy had perpetrated.

The Large Eggs were unanimous in their decision that he must undergo "the punishment" as he had violated the "code of conduct". As the day progressed there was a sense of anticipation in the air. Rumours had spread that something was in the offing and we all waited to see what was going to happen. In reality none of us younger children had ever seen or heard of anyone "breaking the code" and so it was all mysterious and we waited patiently to see what the Large Eggs had in store! In the meantime I thought that Craggy was actually proud of his achievement and had a swagger to his gait. Like us, he was completely unaware of the fate that was to await him.

As he sat on the lawn throwing stones at the sparrows a "posse" of older boys suddenly appeared from nowhere and threw a sack over his head. They manhandled him to his feet and frogmarched him off to the boy scouts hut where they had privacy and Craggy's screams could not be heard. Although only the older boys could be present we found out that Craggy was to stand trial for murdering a chicken.

Presiding over the judgement of the case were John, George and another Large Egg called Fletcher. Eventually Craggy was judged as being guilty as charged and I heard, although I wasn't too sure why he wore it, that John donned a hanky upon his head as the punishment was read out in the court.

According to John he told Craggy, "You will be taken from this court to a place where you will be publicly flogged for your heinous crimes against our feathered friend. After your beating you will report to Sir and apologise for your terrible misdemeanour to his property and then duly receive any further actions that he might want to take. Craggy is that clear?" Craggy then nodded.

He was then strung up to a beam and flogged by all the boys present. He was left to hang for a while before he was cut down and John escorted him to Sir's office to make his confession. We never heard the outcome of his meeting with Sir. Only that Craggy's name was omitted from all further chicken rotas and that he lost privilege entitlements for the next three months.

That, my friend, was punishment Barnardo's style!

A trip to an Aerodrome, our mother pops up again, an unusual gift

Time was moving on and in the autumn of 1952 rumours were beginning to circulate from John and George that our mother was trying to make contact with us again. Although I was beginning to warm to the idea that I may have a mother I was still uncertain just how it should make me feel or how I should respond. I found it difficult to nurture any sort of feelings for a virtually unknown woman and the only real excitement I felt at that time was focused well and truly upon our forthcoming visit to Hooton aerodrome to see one of the very first post-War Air displays. Although the older boys had gone camping earlier in the year to the Isle of Man we were too young to go. Today it was our turn to all go on a trip together. Although we had all seen planes in the air we had never seen an aircraft close up and we were all hoping that today was to be the day to change this. George in particular was mad keen about anything to do with the armed forces and over the years had told us all about how Spitfires and Lancaster Bombers had saved Britain during the War. In fact John reckoned that the RAF defeated the Luftwaffe on their own and Bomber Harris was his own particular hero of the conflict. It was the RAF that caused the Luftwaffe to have to return to Berlin with their tail (fin) between their legs (wings). Today was a great day and we were going to see the aircraft and I was beside myself with excitement.

The bus turned up at the front of Marfords just after we had finished breakfast and so we were excused chores. We piled into the bus, Large Eggs first and Small Eggs last, but the older boys were disinclined to want to sit near to the driver.

George told me that he and John were far too old to play bus-drivers anymore and so they left the front seats exclusively for the kiddy-widdy's. I wasn't really convinced by George's thoughtful gesture and was uncertain whether he was being considerate or sarcastic. I did, however, notice that once the bus was actually moving George and John were more interested in smiling and leering at the young girls out of the rear windows and wondered whether that had anything to do with it. I was surprised that Francis wasn't the least bit interested in being the driver's 2nd mate despite all our goings on at Ashley Coombe.

Suddenly, for just a few minutes, I became aware of how young I was compared to George and John and that they and Francis were changing and yet I was still the same. That my brothers were getting older and growing apart from me and that the times were slowly beginning to change.

During the journey John suddenly stood up on the bus and began to brief us about the Aerodrome. Apparently Hooton Park was originally an RAF station built for the Royal Flying Corps in 1917 as a training aerodrome for pilots in World War I. Nowadays, in the 1950s, No 610 Squadron had reformed along with Supermarine-Spitfire XIVs, then Spitfire 22s, before the Meteor 4 jets. The 663 Squadron formed at Hooton Park in 1949 with Tiger Moths and Auster 5s but were later replaced by de Havilland Chipmunks, and Auster 6s and 7s. I was very impressed that John had done his homework so well, and even the master said that he had done well.

Upon arrival we were all enthralled not only by the sight and smells of the aircrafts but the presence of so many "outsiders". I enquired of the master "why the "outsiders" kept looking at us in that way and also, what was a borstal?" The master asked me about the borstal comment and I told him that Everest and I had overheard somebody saying to their children that, with our suits, we were either orphans or we came from the borstal.

He advised us to ignore their comments and just enjoy ourselves for we were in for an extra special treat that no "outsider" was going to enjoy. Just then an enormous aeroplane flew over. It was so low that it made my hair sweep across my face and it gave me goose-bumps and my teeth chattered in excitement. At 12.30 there was to be Battle of Britain re-enactment with Spitfires, a Wellington and Lancaster Bomber display. We made our way to the demonstration zone just as a number of Spitfires flew over us, turned and lowered their wings at us. They then disappeared for a few minutes before flying in convoy from left to right and heading for an old building in the middle of the zone. Then, they let rip with machine gun fire and had target practice with the buildings.

The noise was ear-cracking and terribly exciting, even overwhelming, for us and we just laughed and clapped at their feats of valour and shouted and just behaved in a way like we had never ever done before. The buildings were left in tatters and some bright spark suggested that they had targeted the wrong dump and in fact that was nurse Nasty's home. It was a sensational event and one that I am sure none of us will have forgotten.

As we stood back to relax we became aware of a very low pitched Buzzing which as it came nearer turned into a roar like a pride of lions all roaring simultaneously. At that moment one of the lads pointed skyward and shouted at us to look up. Well we had never seen such a sight, the sky was so full of bombers that the light seemed to fade as they flew over us. It was absolutely awe-inspiring; such gentle but magnificent giants of the air. They flew past us in a convoy and after several minutes a Lancaster (top image) and a Wellington (lower image, front plane) returned to carry out bombing duty.

In the middle of the field a large white ring was painted, like a bulls-eye, and the bombers took it in turn to target the area with flour bombs to see who could hit closest to the centre of the ring. They must have carried out their reconnaissance, by flying to and fro, on at least three or four occasions before the champion bomber was identified as the Lancaster. The excitement among the crowd was palpable.

Shortly after the demonstrations everybody stood to attention as the military band began to play the National Anthem. The "outsiders", who were standing close by us, seemed to be very surprised that we not only all stood to attention for the King but actually sung the words as well. I was particularly fond of Princess Elizabeth and her family. To me they were a perfect family and I wished that I had a family like them. I had a picture of her in my locker and every night, once the lights were out, I secretly kissed it and whispered "night, night mummy".

As the crowds began to disperse the master called us all over and said that "He had a special treat lined up for us after we had all had a good old cup of Rosie Lea".

"Francis," I said, "what on earth is the master talking about? Rosie who?"

Rather than interrogate anybody we decided that we just follow what the master did and see where it took us. Well it took us to one of the mess rooms where tea had been laid on for us and this was followed by, wait for it, a personal visit for all of us to one of the bombers in the hangar. Well, that was the topping on the cake and we rushed over to enjoy what was to become a once in a lifetime experience. Although we were unaware of the great privilege that we had enjoyed it was almost certainly one of the only occasions when civilian children and their master would have had access to a fully functioning Lancaster bomber. What a memorable outcome for us all and if that wasn't enough, we were all given a post card of the plane itself!

A month later and it was my sixth birthday and I was looking forward to it very much. Over the past few months our mother had begun to resume contact with us again with help from the family support team at Stepney Causeway. Before any visits were officially authorised it was suggested by the teams that a good start would be for her to send us a small treat, on a regular basis, just to start the ball rolling.

Although Francis and I had never seen the parcels from her it appears that she had sent some comics, addressed to her elder son, for all of us. John explained that the comics were actually Martin's and that we were probably too young to understand the stories but as the "cat was now out of the bag" he and George would read them to us.

Francis and I looked inquisitively at each other and together said "Who is Martin?" John explained that he was our new brother, a half-brother and we were going to meet him soon. I started to giggle as I knew that John was pulling my leg.

I looked at him and said "I may be only six now but even I know that our mother could not have another son without a man. Anyway, what do you mean by a half-brother and which half of him is ours?"

John called me "a little thicko" and said "that our mother now had a bloke and that Martin was hers with the bloke hence, he was our half-brother". Well, I did feel this to be very puzzling and wondered what had become of our official real father but John just told me to shut up.

Just before afternoon tea the nurse called all of us into the playroom to tell us that two boxes had arrived from our Mother. One was addressed to me and the second one to us all. We all looked at them in amazement as this was the first time we had ever been sent anything this. They all asked me to open mine first. I frantically ripped at the pretty birthday paper and opened the box to find a lovely big birthday cake. This was the first birthday cake that I had ever had I was really looking forward to scoffing it. It was properly iced and on the top was written, "*Happy Birthday William*" and next to it was a card in which she had written:

"*To my Son William. We hope that you have a lovely birthday and we look forward to seeing you soon. Lots of Love from Mum, Uncle Bill and Martin*".

I looked at John and said "It's true we have another brother and a new Uncle but which Uncle is he?" John suggested that I stop wasting valuable time and let's get on scoffing the cake before it went stale.

"Oh no you don't", said the nurse "This has got to be shared around so that all the boys can celebrate your birthday with you".

I replied that I thought it was unfair as it was for me only and it was my birthday, not there's. Furthermore by the time the cake was cut into all of those pieces there would hardly be enough to taste properly. Unfortunately my protests fell on deaf ears. Our attention then turned to the second box that had been sent to us.

George kept listening intently to it and said that he thought he heard a scuffling coming from within the box. He then enquired "Why did it have "Fragile-Handle with Care" written on the wrapping paper? Nurse decided to open the parcel. She picked it up, opened it at one end and then screamed and put it down on the table. Her face said it all and there was definitely something unusual in it. What exactly had our mother sent us?

She cried out, "There's something alive in it and it was looking at me with beady eyes and with its hideous mouth ajar" she retorted. "It's like a miniature dinosaur or something!

John picked the box up and pulled the creature out, saying "Blimey it's a tortoise, it's a living breathing tortoise. Quick Tubs, that's me, go and fetch some water and grass for it". I wasn't convinced that it was a living creature. It looked more like a lovely crusty pie to me.

"You wouldn't want to sink your greedy little teeth into this Tubs," said John "It's a reptile and it's our pet and look, it has even got its name Peter painted on the shell. Welcome Peter the tortoise to Marfords".

Throughout this time with Peter, as we became acquainted, the nurse looked on in utter disbelief as we were all touching and "cuddling" this ugly, lumpy thingy-me-jig. Her head was nodding from side to side as she said "Well in all my years as a nurse and mother I have never seen anything like this. Fancy, just fancy, sending an animal through the post like it's a book or something."

John reminded her that it wasn't an animal, it was a reptile, and that they love boxes; after all, they live in a shell. Nurse calmed down and after blowing her nose she left us to it saying loudly, as she walked away from us with my cake, "Well I have seen everything now, just about everything".

We were completely unaware, until many years later, that on one particular morning Martin, our new half-brother, awoke to find that his pet tortoise Peter had mysteriously disappeared from his cage. After much wailing and crying and searching it was decided that Peter had escaped and gone walkabout around Walthamstow. Martin later told us that after going through a period of mourning and heartbreak, that lasted for several weeks, he eventually accepted that he would ever find his beloved Peter again.

If I had known about his suffering I might have shed a few crocodile tears on behalf of my unknown half-brother, but overall I would have been pleased that we now had Peter. He was our new family member, even if he was a reptile, whatever one of those was!

Of course we had to ask Sir for permission to keep Peter, which luckily for us was granted, and John made a make-shift cage for him in pride of place by Sir's chicken coop. We were all perfectly happy with this arrangement. It was shortly after Peter had been safely installed in his gardens, and was munching his way through the grass, that my tummy informed me that it must be about the right time for us to also get stuck into my birthday cake!

We scurried back to the dining room and as we entered the boys stood up and sang "Happy Birthday" to me followed by three rousing cheers. I was beaming from ear to ear, not only as a result of my birthday reception but also the thought of scoffing my birthday cake. We all settled down to our usual tea, after which nurse brought the cake out to me with lighted candles blazing away on top of it. I was pleased that the cake was intact and I quickly came to the conclusion that nurse had changed her mind and she was going to let me carve up my own cake. One quarter was for me, one eighth for each for my brothers and the remainder, I didn't have a clue about the maths, for the rest of the boys.

What a really generous birthday boy I thought I was being.

The cake was plonked in front of me in order to blow out the candles but to my horror I realised that rather than being intact it had actually been cut into microscopically narrow wedges. In fact the older boys were taking bets as to whether she had cut it with one of Sir's razor blades or used a cheese wire. Whatever she had done to my cake I was very, very fed up at the miniscule portion that I was about to receive and I told her so. I started to cry and told her that she had ruined my birthday because our Mother had sent the cake for me and not for all the other boys.

As I said that I realised for the first time ever that I had used our mother to "back me up" like this. Anyway, nurse said that I should feel pleased to share my good fortune with those that were less fortunate than us and that our Mother would know what it was like to be without as she was without us right now. She suggested that the best way to show our appreciation of her thoughtfulness would be by sharing her gift with the other poor boys.

Although I was completely "confuddled" by her argument somewhere among the confusion I had to admit some of it seemed to make sense. She was a very persuasive woman. So persuasive in fact that I picked up the plate and offered my cake to each and every boy in the room and I ensured that they all received an equal portion.

That was eating a birthday cake and sharing a birthday - Barnardo style.

At that particular time we were unaware that our time at Marfords was drawing to a close, and in fact, we had only four months or so living there. It seems that the authorities were once again keen for us to meet up with our mother, and shortly after my birthday she was scheduled to visit us. As we were living so far from London that nurse told us that she would be arriving by coach on the Saturday and would spend the night in the sick bay before leaving, after lunch on the Sunday.

When she arrived we were all surprised by two things; first, the punctuality of the coach and second; how young our mother looked compared to the Nurses. I have to say that her entrance was rather theatrical. When we met somebody we would usually remain calm and then extend our hand to shake theirs and say something like "Good morning, madam/sir". Our mother's arrival was in sharp contrast to this.

As she stepped down from the coach she turned, to see us waving on the front steps, and then made a frantic dash for us. Her arms were stretched out towards us and her lips were pursed and smacking together. She appeared to be making a sucking noise with them like a fish at the surface of the water and then as she came closer to us she called out "My babies, my little babies".

I didn't want her to kiss me with those odd lips and what's more I wasn't a baby. I, was almost a man now! Once the drama of her arrival had subsided we made our way together to the playroom. In the meantime the other boys were asked to play on the lawns.

Suddenly she turned around to face us, delved into her bag and pulled out a tin of something. I thought that it was a magic trick that she was performing and clapped, but John said "I was being silly and that I should not try to be the centre of attention all the time".

Anyway she pulled back a ring on the top of the can to reveal some odd yellow rings in liquid. "These" she said proudly, "are pineapple rings and you cannot get these for love or money. So try one they are a real treat." At that she stuck her finger into the can and offered us each one of the yellow things. Somehow she had managed to place her finger into the centre of the pineapple ring so that as she extracted her hand, away from the can, it looked like a large yellow lump of jewellery on her index finger.

I was able to eat for England at any time and had a reputation for my scoffing ability but even I really didn't fancy trying this. Whether I was concerned about how clean her finger was or the appearance and smell of the pineapple I wasn't too sure. In the end we all tried it but thought it was revolting. We had never seen, smelled or tasted anything like it before and so it was immediately shunned by us. George was so convinced that she was trying to poison us that he threatened to fetch the nurse.

Francis and I were keen to show her our dormitory and as the other boys were playing outside we took her to see it. "Is this where you hang your clothes then, Billy and Francis?" said mum, looking at the wardrobe in the corner.

In fact we were not allowed to use it and it was scheduled to be removed from our dorm. When our mother opened the door of the wardrobe to look inside Francis invited her to get in, an odd request but she did it, whereupon he closed the door. He then told me to help him to push it over. The wardrobe fell onto its door and became propped up against a bed. She was effectively trapped inside.

To be honest I was very shocked at our actions and was unable to explain why we had done such an awful thing. For the first time I began to feel a sense of responsibility for my actions and that things that seem like fun could turn out very badly. I was now beginning to feel some sort of rapport with our mother as well as sympathy as she lay screaming at the top of her voice in the wardrobe. In fact we were unable to free her and had to fetch the master to help us pick the wardrobe up. The master looked at us all and said "I don't want to spoil your mother's visit today but I will deal you all after she has returned home!"

Our mother was very shaken by our escapade but, although I sensed that she was really angry with us and also upset by our unkindness to her, she didn't let it show. On the contrary she behaved as though nothing had happened despite the bruise to her arm and the scratches on her face. Maybe it was the sense of guilt that I was feeling from my inconsiderate actions but feelings for my mother were now beginning to emerge. After we waved her off the next day, I have to say, that I was looking forward to her return visit.

Health issues and the time to move on yet again.

It was during a routine medical check-up, which we were all put through from time to time, that it came to light that the doctor had some concerns over Francis. Apparently he was failing to thrive, was underweight for his age and his skin was in poor shape, particularly his upper torso. Francis had already acquired the nickname "map-chest" by some of the older boys because of all the veins that could be seen through his thin skin. In fact one of the boys reckoned that his chest looked like a London underground map. Anyway the doctor recommended that he receive the latest health innovation 'Sunray' therapy. Sunray therapy UV-lamps became a popular remedy in the 1950s when doctors became convinced that the treatment would have a curative effect on a range of conditions. Francis began weekly sessions, sometimes when sitting in the sick room or, when the weather was warmer, in the garden sun-house with the lamp shining upon his body. The nurse would then periodically rotate the sun-house to ensure that Francis received the rays from the sun as well as from the lamp.

Although I had the all-clear from the doctor, on that occasion, it was shortly afterwards that I began to feel unwell. The first symptom that I developed was a loss of appetite, usual for me so the nurse kept special eye on me. As the days progressed I became more and more listless and I developed a temperature and at that stage I was put into quarantine in the sick bay. That night my tongue and skin felt odd and I had very bad headache. By the time Nurse returned to see me she became very concerned and called the doctor. He suggested that it was measles and that I should be kept in isolation and that he would return the next day.

Overnight my situation had worsened and it was agreed that I should be admitted into hospital as an emergency. I began to feel very anxious as the team talked about me being taken to the Liverpool Royal Infirmary by ambulance. Some of the boys said that I was lucky to be going in an ambulance and that I would not have to put up with school for the foreseeable future. I wasn't really paying attention to their chit-chat. I felt too unwell.

I can remember the ambulance taking me to the hospital with the big bell ringing out and the doctors fussing over me and taking my temperature and checking upon my ears. When we arrived I was taken immediately to an isolation ward which was very dimly lit as the light hurt my eyes.

Twice a day the nurse appeared with the largest syringe that I had ever seen. The sight of her holding it terrified me and I screamed out in sheer fear. In the end the Nurse recruited the help of two men to restrain me and expose my rear-side for the injection. It was a strong antibiotic that was needed to deal with a serious middle ear infection that I had acquired as a result of having measles.

That night I took a turn for the worse and my head felt as though it was about to explode. One of the nurses called for the hospital chaplain to come to see me. I remember he was dressed in purple and they both prayed for me as did the children back at the "Marfords" and at my school. I must have been in a very bad way because I later found out that the chaplain had administered the Last Rites to me.

For the next day or two everyone waited with bated breath to see whether the treatment was working and whether the infection was in fact subsiding. Fortunately for me it had and the doctor reckoned that the infection had left me with permanent damage to my left ear. I had been left with a perforation in my left eardrum, which would make me susceptible to ear infections from then on. Also as the small bones in the ear, the ossicles, were irreparably damaged leaving me partially deaf.

My life was changed for ever. These complications with my ear were to blight my life throughout my adolescence and young adulthood. The good news, however, was that I was soon back and reunited with my brothers. All was well again and it felt good to be back, feeling better and safe with them. After the excitement of our reunion all I wanted to do was to see Peter the tortoise again and tell him of my most recent adventure and close encounters.

It was now early in 1953 and we were told the news that we had been anticipating for some time. Our mother was keen to visit us on a more regular basis and John and George were now too old to remain at the Marfords. The family support team thought the time was now appropriate for us to be placed in a residential home closer to the London area in order to facilitate her visits. The time had come to move on and our final residential home was New Lodge, near Windsor in Berkshire, where we arrived in February 1953. Goodbye Bromborough - Hello Windsor.

CHAPTER THREE

Army barmy (an aside) and an Introduction

I was never sure where it came from or who donated it and so the gift that I received will remain a mystery to me for ever. It was in the aftermath of my illness, just before we were scheduled to move on to New Lodge, when a made-to-measure army uniform appeared, folded up on the top of my locker, next to my bed. It has always remained a great sadness that I was never able to personally thank my benefactors for their tremendous kindness. How were they to know that this uniform would focus my heart upon a career in the army and that I would become a regular soldier? Or so I thought I would!

I was absolutely smitten with my gift and refused to take it off. I would march around in it and bark orders at the civilians in my dorm. To say that I fell in love with the thought of an army life would be an understatement. I even refused to take the uniform off for my last few days at the local school. When I did take it off, at night, I secreted it under my mattress so that nobody would nick it.

In hindsight I guess that the staff had been told to cut us all some slack in our last few days at Marfords as nobody, not even Sir, challenged me or reprimanded me for wearing unauthorised or non-approved clothing. To me the trousers, jacket and beret were so authentic that "outsiders" must have thought that I was a regular soldier and wearing them made me feel as proud as punch.

For the first time in my life I felt a real sense of independence from Barnardo's and the regime by wearing something of my choice and not of theirs. Also, for the first time, I no longer felt that I was not part of a quartet but was, in fact, an individual with my own thoughts and ideas. I guess that this was me beginning to grow up! From that period of time onwards I thought of nothing else but joining the army as soon as I had the chance.

I supposed that such a notion, as joining up, was not that unusual when one considers my background. Analysts would probably make a case for my military yearnings and desires as being my search for the closeness of a tight family unit. I didn't quite see myself in that light at the time. All I knew was that I liked the idea of becoming a soldier.

By the time I had almost reached my teen years I had been back home, with our mother, for several years. On a regular basis I would venture down to the Army Cadet Force, the First Essex Regiment based at Chingford Barracks, hankering to be admitted, despite being underage. I would just hang around the hall watching the other cadets and wishing that I was one of them. I was transfixed upon joining.

One evening the recruiting Sergeant came over to me, as I was loitering with intent to join, and told me that if I came back with a letter from my mother permitting me to join under age he would see about it. Actually, at that time, I was twelve and a half, just six months too young. To get passed this hurdle I went home and wrote a letter to that effect myself, and when I turned up the following week he said "Right Tyrrell, you are in" and my dreams had come true.

Over the coming months and years I never missed a meeting. I went to every annual camp, loved every minute and became a crack marksman. I was setting myself up for a real career in the army.

In 1961, when I was fifteen years of age and with a fantastic letter of recommendation from the Cadet force, I embarked on my dream to join the Junior Leaders. I passed every conceivable test that they threw at me to prove that I could think and speak for myself, do sums and solve problems. All that I faced now was the medical, the dreaded medical.

The doctor looked down my left ear and did a double take. He rubbed his eyes in apparent disbelief at what he had seen and then looked at me and said "Good God man, are you aware of the fact that you have a perforated eardrum".

"A perforated what" I replied.

"A perforated eardrum in your left ear Sonny. It's in a terrible bloody state. Surely you knew that didn't you"? he retorted

"I knew that I had a little problem with my ear but I never realised that it was that bad. Do you think it will affect my chances of getting in Sir only this has been my heart's desire since I was six years old" I replied.

"There is no way that you can get into this or any other army. You might squeeze in, peeling the spuds during a major conflict, but otherwise there is no way in for you. Sorry Son".

I was devastated by this terrible news. My one opportunity had slipped through my hands and I returned home to lick my wounds, seek solace from my brothers and re-evaluate my life.

In the meantime back to 1952 and our arrival at New Lodge (below).

As you can see New Lodge was a large country house set in 55 acres of open countryside to the west of Windsor Great Park. It was built in about 1857, in Jacobean style, for Jean-Sylvain Van de Weyer, a Belgian politician who served as the Belgian ambassador to the United Kingdom.

In 1942 the property was acquired by Barnardo's for £24,000 and used as a residential home for boys until 1956 when the building was purchased by the British Transport Commission and used as a training school for railway catering staff.

The first reunion of ex-Barnardo boys who lived at New Lodge between the years 1950 to 1955, the period that included us, was arranged in 1992. It seemed to us, from first impressions, that New Lodge was run in a similar way to Marfords, but within a day or two of our arrival we discovered that we were mistaken. John and George were housed in one dormitory and Francis and I in another ours was enormous with very high ceilings and wooden tiled floors. We were awoken at 6.30 am by the sound of the bugle, which in time John learned to play. In addition we were told to wear working clothes only while we were indoors, and every morning we had half an hour's chores to do before breakfast. In that respect it was quite reassuring to have continuity with Marfords.

Settling in, new regimes and some behavioural problems

The Monday after our arrival it was decided that we should each resume our schooling again. Being the youngest boy in the home I was taken to Bray Wood Infant School all on my own and was driven to the school by one of the masters. Francis, George and John were taken, by coach to Royal Free School for Boys in Windsor. I would rather have gone with them altogether in the coach as it seemed like much more fun. In the afternoon one of the masters would return to escort me back to New Lodge again, often walking cross-country.

It came as no surprise to us that within the first week or so of our arrival an official Barnardo photograph was taken of us. This picture, of the four of us, was taken by the steps that go down to the lawn. John and George are standing (top right and left) with me (front left) and Francis. You can see that my school tie is different to the one that they were wearing and that Francis is being good and showing the world that he had a clean hankie in his pocket. I am not too sure whether the suits that we were wearing were our regulation school uniform or the official Barnardo's uniform. Either way they were very itchy and classified as "outdoor" clothing only which meant that they were never to be worn indoors.

Shortly after this photograph was taken we met the new Superintendent at New Lodge. In comparison to Old Winkle the new Sir, Mr. Macey, was really quite scary and very, very authoritative. At our initial meeting with him Francis and I both were both mesmerised by his spectacles, I had never seen such thick rims and the lenses appeared to have been made out of the bottom of milk bottles. They looked hideous and from where we were standing they made his eyes look like big white boiled eggs. Frank whispered to me about "frog-eyes" and I replied that he was "eggy-eyed". He reminded us that he would not accept rude or disrespectful behaviour from any boys and then introduced us to a few of the masters. We were soon to lock horns with two of them over the coming days.

During this settling-in period, at New Lodge, one of the older boys warned John and George, who in turn warned us, to be on the look-out for Lugwig. He was one of the masters that we met earlier and he was most feared by the other boys. They reckoned that he was a "nasty bit of business and that it's best to avoid him at all times". John wasn't really too sure what his confidante had meant by this description of Lugwig but it didn't take too long before we were to find out, especially, how he had acquired such a reputation.

Although there were some regimes at Marfords, bugle call in the morning, marching to the bell and daily chores, this place had much more formality about it. In addition there were several regimes, as will soon come to light, that reflected the Victorian notion of childcare in terms of being completely archaic and inconsistent with modern trends in childcare and welfare found in Barnardo's today.

For a start I was only allowed to dress in my army uniform in the playroom. I wasn't allowed outside with it on as we were only permitted to wear approved "outside" clothing. I was very miffed by this and sulked about it for days. I thought that even if I held my breath for evermore they would not let me have my own way; they were a load of rotter's! Another of the archaic regimes was daily shoe inspection!

As in our previous homes the cleaning of shoes was compulsory. We now, however, had to clean our shoes in a very particular way every day before school or before we went on an outing. Not only did we clean and polish the uppers of our shoes, until they shone like the sun, but we also had do with the same with the in-steps. We were only aware of this ridiculous chore once we had joined the queue ready for Lugwig's shoe inspection. To be frank with you we were all surprised that Sir would deem it necessary for us to undertake such a useless chore especially just before we were due to leave for school.

The routine went something along these lines: once we had finished polishing our shoes we were made to form an orderly inspection line in the corridor. Lugwig would stand at the front of the queue, under the big wall clock, to carry out his examination of them. As one reached the front of the queue he would look at the uppers of the shoes. If they were shining to an acceptable degree he would then gesticulate, in a circular clockwise motion with his index finger, for you to turn them over to reveal the soles of your shoes. The experienced boys were dab-hand at doing this, in one simple rotation of their wrist, but for us it took a little practice.

If you were one of the unfortunate enough to fail the inspection, as Francis and I certainly were in our earlier days at New Lodge, Lugwig would grab you by the ear, hence his "nom de plume" Lugwig, spin you around and slap the back of your legs whilst chanting "Warm legs Sonny Jim, warm legs".

I did tell you that the regimes were outdated and archaic!

I squealed out to him, "My name is not Sonny Jim its William". He replied, "More warm legs Sonny Jim, more warm legs".

I thought that this punishment regime was completely over the top, even brutal for such a minor oversight. Such bullying, coupled with him calling me Sonny Jim, bought to mind the infamous nurse Nasty, of the soap in the mouth trick as well as the sweetie shop keeper, of gobstopper fame. After Lugwig's shoe inspection we returned to our dorm, in order to prepare for school, and then have breakfast.

My early school memories of Windsor are rather limited on two accounts. The first was my predisposition to daydream for most of the day. A second, and more worrying condition, was a new and sudden pre-occupation associated with all of the goings on in my life. I thought about the move to New Lodge, the abandonment of my army uniform, the harshness of some of the masters and now John reckoned that our mother wanted to visit us more frequently with the view that we might all be repatriated back to her again. How was I possibly to think about learning, reciting my times-table or singing about "Little Robin Redbreast sitting upon a tree" when my head was filled with so much other "stuff".

One evening Francis and I were both in our dormitory and talking about our situation and looking to console and support each other. As we were speaking to each other one of the other boys decided that it would be a great hoot to throw a pillow in our direction. Now although Francis was of a smallish stature he was, nevertheless, quite "wound up" and had developed a warrior mentality. Nobody was going to pick on him and get away with it! With that frame of mind he wasn't going to take any lip from anybody. He picked the pillow up and walloped it as hard as he could across the chops of the perpetrator. Justice had been done!

Unfortunately, that was not the end of the matter and despite the fact that the "lights out" bugle had sounded we had an almighty dormitory pillow fight. I was having a wonderful time and every smack of the pillow onto somebody's bonce really helped to subdue the anxieties that I had. I suppose the racket that we were making must have alerted the masters and shortly afterwards the door flew open and they entered mob-handed. They looked around in utter disbelief at the carnage that we had all inflicted and they ordered us to all to stand up, form an orderly queue and then march down to the main hall.

On the way down there I whispered to Francis that we were now in a serious situation, but one of the masters, Snowy, named after the colour of his hair, told us "to shut up and to keep quiet".

As we entered the hall we were told to line up against the long wall by Sir's office. What's more we had to stand with our hands behind our backs and with our noses touching the wall directly under the old wall clock.

"This," said the master, "is the fate of all boys who err and stray from the rules. It's, stand under the clock time". He then left us on our own.

I said to Francis "why we were standing like this" and he reckoned that "Sir was going to make us wait under the clock so that as the time passed we would all think about our individual part in the misdemeanour, regret our participation and then receive our punishment though surely this was punishment enough?"

After, what seemed to be hours, each boy was called into the office by Sir. From the atmosphere in the hall we could all sense what was going on. We could hear a garbled muffled noise rather like a fat juicy bluebottle buzzing around in a jam-jar, followed by a thwack, thwack, thwack, then a crying-out followed by the door opening and

Sir shouting out "Now get out of here and don't show your nose around this hall ever again. Is that clear boy?" In a way I felt rather smug as I was only six years and eight months old and I felt that he wouldn't cane me. Would he?

Eventually I was the only one left behind and I was called in. I was really quite terrified but Sir did not hesitate to haul me over the desk and give me three of the best on my backside. I cried and wailed out aloud and then rushed back to the dorm to see Francis. Unfortunately Mr Macey decided that to prevent any further mischief he would personally wait in our dorm until we were all fast asleep.

With a very sore backside, from the caning, sore and red eyes, from the crying and unable to speak to Francis, because of old Macey, I crawled into bed and fell asleep.

I would like to say that this uncharacteristic behaviour pattern should have "knocked it out of us" with each thwack of the cane. You would have thought that I would have learned my lesson and kept to the straight and narrow from then on. That was, in fact, my intention to keep my nose clean, to act with more caution and under no circumstances get into Sir's "bad-book" again. As I entered my school the next day I felt quite pleased with myself as I had passed the shoe inspection, first time, done my chores satisfactorily and had a hearty breakfast. It is true to say that John was displeased that Francis and I had both been caned and were effectively under house arrest, for the time being, but I was confident about the day ahead of me.

That was, however, before I was seduced by the most amazing sight that I had ever seen in my life. My seduction occurred when I returned to school and was seated at my desk. It was definitely a case of "love at first sight". The love of my life came with very sleek contours and a beautiful smooth surface which brought a yearning of such intensity that I could not resist the challenge that was set before me. As I sat down at my desk I couldn't help but notice that the boy sitting next to me had the most amazing and beautiful plastic toy knife in his desk. I just kept staring at it, it made my heart race and my pulse increase, I just could not take my eyes off of it. I had to have it! I was mesmerised by its sheer beauty and wanted it in my possession by hook or by crook.

In reality we had very little that we could call our own. I guess that my brothers were the only thing in my life that measured up to being mine and mine only. Now I wanted that knife.

I asked the lad if I might take a closer look at his knife just to feel what it was like to be in my own hands. I was very disappointed by his reaction and I thought that he was very beastly and unfriendly. He kept saying nasty things to me and taunting me. He then reckoned that kids like me, from homes, didn't deserve anything like this and that I wouldn't be able to afford anything like it anyway. Just to rub salt into my "wounds of disappointment" he made my yearning even greater as, unbeknown to me, his knife had a very special and unique feature the like of which I had never seen before.

He held the blade over his open hand and then appeared to stab himself. I was ashen. However he then pulled the knife out and there was no injury or blood visible. I was transfixed by this but he continued to laugh at me. As it happened, and to my utter amazement, the blade actually retracted back into the handle of the knife upon impact. The blade was spring loaded and, in fact, he hadn't stabbed himself at all. I was absolutely besotted with his possession and wanted it for myself.

I decided that if he wasn't going to let me share it, or at least have a go with it, then I would nick it. I would make my move on it during playtime when the class was empty.

Then the deed was done.

During playtime I went into the toilet alone and sat there admiring it and playing with my new acquisition. After playtime the bell rang for us to return back to class when I suddenly began to panic. What was I to do? The knife was made to scale and I realised that had very few places, if any, to conceal it about myself? I guess the sensible thing to have done would have been to confess to my moment of weakness and to tell Sir what I did on the spur of the moment. Alternatively I could have hidden the knife in the toilet and, if it was discovered the finger of blame may not necessarily have been pointed in my direction. However being rather naive I didn't really think that I would be caught and so I decided to conceal it down my woollen sock and return back to my class.

I was beginning to think that I had got away with my crime when suddenly the classroom door burst open and in walked the Headmaster, accompanied with a school prefect. The master immediately stopped the lesson and we all looked intently towards the Head in anticipation of what he might have had to say to us! I was convinced that my crime was to be rumbled and that this was going to be a public humiliation for me. Sir looked around at us all and told us that he had just received some very distressing news that one of our class members had a personal item removed from his desk during the break. He then suggested that it would be good for all of us if the person responsible were to own up to this misdemeanour.

As I sat at my desk I became ever more convinced that my involvement was visible for all to see as my face was glowing like a light bulb with guilt. I was now in a real quandary. On the one hand, I honestly felt that I deserved to own a wonderful possession, but, on the other hand, I realised that my actions were wrong and whatever I did I was going to suffer in one way or another. Under the circumstances I decided not to do or say anything and the die was cast.

We were told to lift up our desk lids and he gestured to the prefect to search each one for the missing item. Of course I was confident that he would be unsuccessful and he must have reported this to the masters. They had a conversation amongst themselves before he asked each child to stand and walk to the front of the class. They started with the children in the first row and I was seated in the fourth row. As they went to the front each child was asked to turn around on the spot. It was clear that this was all they needed to do because the knife was so large it was virtually impossible to conceal completely.

I knew as I made the "walk of shame" to the front my fate was sealed. This, indeed, is precisely what happened, for as I ventured up I could hear gasps from some of the children and one or two of them were actually pointing at my sock. This is it, I thought to myself; the best thing that I could now do, in order to maintain any kind composure, was not to show any weakness and definitely not to cry. So that was it. My "get of jail free" card was to ensure that under no circumstances would my classmates see me cry. No tears, no sign of weakness.

The Headmaster addressed the class to remind them that theft was a serious crime and that thieves always get punished. He told me to put out my hand and I offered him my open palm whereupon he administered three thwacks directly onto it. I actually felt pleased with myself because I didn't flinch or shed a tear.

This was a new experience for me and although I was not proud of my actions I wasn't sorry for the boy in the next desk and certainly felt that I was somehow revered by the others for not showing any weakness. This notion of acquiring a reputation for being brave and stoical was something I enjoyed, as with it comes respect and that was something else that I was keen to acquire. After the cane I was told to stand in the corner until my chaperone arrived to take me back to New Lodge.

I suppose in one way I was more concerned that I might get further grief and punishment upon my return to New Lodge but they say "fortune favours the brave". Well I had been brave as I had not cried.

As we began to walk back the master said to me "Tyrrell what was all that about?"

I told him that I had done something stupid and stolen a boy's knife, that I had been caught and received three of the best on the palm of my hand.

He asked me "whether I had learned my lesson and said that theft was a despicable act".

I replied "that I couldn't really help myself after all we were all used to sharing things in New Lodge".

He then reminded me that I had not answered his question. "Did you regret your actions or not?" I replied "that I did".

"Well we will not discuss this ever again Tyrrell. Now what kind of birds can you see in that field?"

That was that. It was never discussed again!

A new boy and some very rude "developments"!

Over the next few weeks life went on as usual as I attempted to put the incident with the knife behind me. I found it difficult to "pick up the pieces" in my relationships with the other lads at school. They did not shun me, or anything like that, it was just that I was not invited into their groups. In a strange way it seemed as though I was not one of them and although I never sensed this before the incident I certainly felt it afterwards. As far as the victim was concerned it was decided that he should move to a new desk and that was really the end of our association. I suppose that you could say that I made a conscious decision not to raise my head too far above the parapet and that included my contributions to the learning situation in the classroom. I had learned my lesson and was now determined not to get the cane again.

It was a bit of relief for me really when one morning as, I arrived in the playground, I noticed that we had a new boy. At least, I thought to myself, he would deflect the attention away from me. As I stood alone in the playground I looked at him and tried to "suss him up" in terms of whether he might be a likely friend or foe. For reasons, that I am really unable to explain, I decided upon the former, possibly, because my first impression was that he was not like the other "outsiders". To me he seemed more like an "insider", appearing to be wearing the "I'm from an institution" tag but not one from New Lodge.

I was really quite intrigued. I couldn't quite put my finger on what it was about him that was so different whether it was his dress sense (a bit scruffy), his deportment (he seemed a little scrunched up), or his general demeanour, but I definitely sensed that, like me, he was different. I have to say that my first impression of him was very accurate.

I plucked up the courage to go over to him and say "Hello are you a new boy then?"

As soon as he said that he was, my self-enquiries were answered; he was a foreigner. I had never ever met anybody who didn't come from home, apart from Everest, so I wanted to know more. He spoke English quite well but his accent was very strong.

"What is your name then? I am William," I said.

He replied that "his name was Anthony and that he had come here from Germany with his mother and father".

Blimey, I thought, perhaps he is a spy?

I told him "that my eldest brother John also had the name Anthony, as his middle name, and that my middle name was Patrick".

We seemed to hit it off almost immediately as if there was some connection between us, and in true Barnardo fashion, I stretched out my hand and we shook on our new found friendship.

I was pleased that I had befriended him because I was pretty sure that the other boys would probably not want to associate with a German boy. Most of us had some understanding of the Second World War; after all some goods like sweets were still on ration, and hostilities towards Germany continued throughout Europe. Actually, in the classroom situation Anthony was really bright and could read and write a lot better than many of us. I thought that he might have been my age but he was considerably more knowledgeable and I remember thinking Blimey, at what age do they start school over there? While they are still in nappies?

Over the coming weeks we learned a lot about each other. I felt that the main connection between us was centred upon our disrupted backgrounds and the uncertainty that this created in terms of instability and continuity in life. Yes, as far as I was concerned there was definitely a form of bond that cemented our relationship.

I decided then that anyone who wanted to take a pop at Anthony would have to take a pop at me first. As I was the boy that failed to cry when they were caned I felt pretty confident that Anthony would not get his feathers ruffled by any of the other boys.

One day Anthony mentioned that his family were sent over here as displaced persons after the war and he went on to explain that his family home in Germany was no longer in their possession. Furthermore he reckoned that his family were living in some form of a camp that was operated by the British Army before they were sent here on a resettlement programme. I wasn't really too sure how to react to what Anthony told me but their plight sounded awful. I mentioned to John and George that I had met Anthony and that he was a misplaced person from Germany and I asked them to explain to me exactly what a misplaced person was.

John said to me that "Anthony was, in fact, displaced and not misplaced.

A displaced person is somebody who is forced to move to another country because of war or persecution and is seeking 'refuge', a safe place to stay. A misplaced person is different having a home to go to but being unable to find it".

John then asked me "if Anthony was in fact a German or someone from another country other than Germany."

In time I discovered that Anthony's parents were German Jews and that he could speak German, some English and Yiddish, whatever language that was. One day, as we were playing in the school playground, I told Anthony that I might be returning back to London and asked him whether he would be returning back to Germany once he had finished at the school.

Anthony told me "that it was very unlikely as he had nowhere to go in Germany".

"Oh Anthony", I replied, "I am sorry to hear that. Perhaps you will come and see me when I return to London".

Anthony impressed me a lot especially, his demeanour and general attitude in the face of the hardship, which he and his family had endured. They were real heroes who had suffered terrible hardship and prejudice through no fault of their own, just as I had done. I could readily identify with this characteristic of their lives.

Over the coming weeks Anthony taught me, what he called, some of his survival skills, which he had been taught earlier on in his life back home. They included drinking water from puddles and eating certain kinds of leaves. I suggested to him that it might be inappropriate to practise such skills in our playground as the others might find it a bit weird. It did not connect with me that for Anthony and his family these were essential survival skills which enabled them to endure their ordeal. This was a positive time for me at school, and through our backgrounds Anthony and I found a common link. Our lives had been enriched by our association and, as a result, this was a really meaningful time in my young life and I was never to forget my friendship with him.

Back at New Lodge another of Mr Macey's new regimes was a weekly fire drill. This would occur at any time of the night and on random evenings. In order to ensure that we arrived at the correct assembly point it was essential that we kept our kit folded together, in a small pile, and secured with the snake belt. We then had to place it at the bottom of the bed. In that way we could pick up our clothes, assemble in our jim-jams but still go to school because we had our clothes with us all of the time. The two nurses in the adjacent room would then accompany us during the drill. It seemed to me that, once the alarm bell sounded, it was we boys that would form an orderly queue, march to the assembly point and be ready for roll call while the nurses and master remained flustered and panic-stricken throughout. Anyway, after roll call we would make our way back to our dorms and return to sleep.

Overall it was just a bit of fun for us.

One afternoon, having just returned from school, I went directly to the dorm to change into my "indoor" togs when, to my surprise, I found Francis in the dorm as well. Apparently he reckoned that he wasn't feeling too well that morning and had a temperature and so the master suggested that he stay behind in bed.

He went on tell me that the nurse came in every hour to take his temperature and that he had discovered that her room, which she shared with another nurse, was adjacent to our dorm. He had also discovered that if he peeped through the key hole he could see them in their room.

I suggested that his new hobby was, in fact, very wrong and he shouldn't be peeping at them. I told him that if he was caught he would be severely reprimanded. Anyway I liked that nurse as she was one of the few really nice ones and I told him so. I said that "she had been kind to me by helping me with my reading and taking me to the library.

"So what?" he said "We are only having a harmless look. Anyway if you are too prissy you don't have to look if you don't want to".

Well I didn't want him to consider me as prissy and so I joined in with his jape. Later that day, while we were alone in the dorm Francis got down on one knee and began peeping through the keyhole. In the meantime I kept digs for him.

"What can you see? What can you see?" I whispered to him. "Not much" replied Francis, "But we might have better luck later on."

After tea we were both allowed to return to the dorm on the pretext that I needed to help Francis prepare for an early night due to his temperature during the day. We quickly resumed our positions whereupon Francis gasped and called to me "Blimey, one of them is undressing and she's got some really strange garments".

"Let me see, Francis. It's my turn. I want to see all the funny clobber as well," I replied.

Francis then reported back "that one of them was walking towards the other door and had left the room".

The next thing I knew our door suddenly flew open and one of the nurses grabbed me by the ear and asked me what I was doing.

"Who me Mam? Why nothing, I was standing here minding my own business," I replied.

"What about you Francis? Were you peeping at us in our room? Cos if you were you will be in deep trouble," said the nurse.

"Actually, it's not quite what it seems, Mam" he retorted "We actually thought the room was unoccupied and then, suddenly, during the day, I heard noises and thought that somebody was up to no good in there.

That's all Mam. I was just checking it out. Better to be safe than sorry".

Well I would like to think that was our only deviant act. In fact, technically, I did not peep; it was Francis that did all of the peeping and I just kept digs to ensure that he wasn't caught red-handed. There was, however, more to follow, and this time it involved all of the boys in our dorm. In the meantime some appropriate tape suddenly appeared covered the crucial keyhole. That put paid to our pranks.

One Sunday afternoon Francis and I were playing with George and John and some of the older boys in the playroom. They kept complaining about the chores they were having to do. Their main complaint was focussed upon polishing the floor of the toilets using a special red polish soaked into a bumper. The polish was called Ronuk and it was the most vivid red colour that I had ever seen.

Looking back I am pretty sure that the older boys were intending to have some great fun at our expense. They knew that by telling me their secret and asking me not to reveal it to anybody on the pain of death that, gobby little me, would tell all and sundry about it. Which of course I did. I whistled like a lark in the sky. The other Little Eggs, like butter in my hands, were keen to get involved at any expense.

Well according to John, "Ronuk was not only brilliant, at polishing the floor to a great sparkle, but it had another, less well known property, especially if you were a man".

"What do you mean" I asked

"Well," said John, "if you rub it liberally over your, 'you know what', it grows and expands very quickly just like a real man".

I then asked John "if he knew whether my 'you-know-what' was anywhere near to my, 'you-know-where'? To be frank I didn't have a clue what he was on about.

All of the Large Eggs looked at me and in unison said that your 'you-know-what', was actually my John Thomas".

Well, I was even more confused now because I was not only unsure where my 'you-know-what' was but I didn't even know what or where my John Thomas was either.

"Anyway" I asked "how do you know that I've even got a 'you-know-what' or a John Thomas come to that."

"Because all of us have one stupid" they replied

At that point Francis intervened in order to prevent me from making a fool of myself in front of all of the big eggs. He sidled up to me and whispered into my ear "that they were referring to my winkle".

I was really taken back by this however I was also concerned about my naivety and wondered why I wasn't as "street wise" as they were! Anyway I thought that the idea was ridiculous but, much to my surprise, when I told the others about it, back at the dorm, they were all up for trying it out. What's more they all knew exactly what I meant when I said that they had to rub the Ronuk onto their 'you-know-what'.

Although I was somewhat suspicious of the intentions of the older boys, I decided that I couldn't back-out of their escapade as all of the other Small Eggs were so keen to give it a go. As a result I followed them like a lamb to the slaughter. Acting against my better judgment, I joined the queue of young boys all lined up with their trousers around their ankles, liberally spreading this red polish all over their private parts. Actually it was both funny to watch us and enjoyable, in a weird sort of way, as we were bonding together. As we were all enjoying the revelry of our actions the older boys came down to spy on us and have a very good laugh at our expense.

They could hardly contain themselves when one of them asked whether it was working or not. Unfortunately that was a story that wasn't going to be silenced very easily and the Large Eggs must have "dined out" on it for many a month. I can't really blame them for their fun, after all, we were the stupid bunch of twits that fell for it and we deserved everything that occurred in the aftermath. Later that week we had some real explaining to do especially when we went swimming and the master wanted to know why all of us had red dye smeared all over our lower parts. It makes me cringe now to think of the humiliation I felt having to explain myself away and God knows what the master thought of us all. Having said that, even today, the image in my mind of we little kids frantically rubbing red polish into ourselves in the hope that we would suddenly be hung like a stallion still brings a great big smile to my face. In the end the older boys should have been congratulated for thinking up such a wonderful prank to play upon their younger counterparts.

That was having fun and jolly japes Barnardo's style.

Sunny Holiday greetings from Devon

Once a year the boys at New Lodge were taken on holiday to Devon. Although George and John had previously been on holiday to the Isle of Man this was to be our first and Francis and I were both very excited at the prospect. We were informed by Mr Macey that all of the boys would be going along with three or four of the masters and that we would be staying in a resort called Brixham, in Devon for two weeks.

On the morning of our departure we all assembled by the front lawn, in our "outdoor" clothing, and each of us carried a small valise containing the rest of our belongings. A coach picked us up and took us to the station for our onward journey by train. We were all too excited to have any real idea of the route we were taking or really where the resort actually was. My main concern, once we were all settled in our carriage with a master, was when I was going to be fed as I had acquired quite an appetite through all of the excitement.

Our master, fully aware of the consequences if he filled our tummies with goodies while we were so exuberant, simply said nothing about our lunch until we had calmed down and were sitting still. Then, we were each given a packed lunch. I had never faced such a dilemma before as I could actually pick and choose precisely what I wanted to eat from a selection of goodies that made this little piggy squeak with glee. Best of all we could swap with each other as well. This was not only going to be my first experience of being by the seaside and of staying in a local school but now I had experienced the pleasure and delight of a packed lunch. To me this had all the joy of picking out a lucky dip from the local sweet shop. After we had taken it in turns to peek out of the window to look at the colour of the coachwork of our carriage we played I-Spy for a while and then most of us took an afternoon nap on the velvety seats.

When we arrived at Brixham Station our master told us to remain seated with our valises on our laps until we could hear the porter's whistle. At that point we all jumped up, opened the carriage door and made a dash for the "little room". It had been quite a long and tiring journey. After our comfort break we all reassembled at the front of the station when I noticed John and George in deep conversation and decided to join them so that I could "earwig".

What's up then?" I asked.

They were just standing there admiring the train and going on about how beautiful it was and what a great way it was to travel. At that point we were told to queue in our year groups and for us to follow the Large Eggs down to the school which was to be our home for the next two weeks. On the way down one of the older boys began to whistle a tune which was unfamiliar to me at the time but was to become resonant during our time at Brixham. Funnily enough some of the other boys started giggling and whispering some words to accompany the tune. I thought that as they were giggling there was going to be something untoward in their lyrics and although I couldn't quite make the words out I soon realised that I was correct in my assumption. It became obvious that one of the masters was familiar with the song and that it had some unsavoury meaning for he shouted out to them "to stop the noise immediately or there would be trouble in store". Thank goodness that I wasn't involved in it.

Upon our arrival we received a very warm welcome from a group of old ladies who were not only expecting us as their guests, but, had prepared supper for us. Ah! Food. Now that was guaranteed to make me very happy.

We were shown to our dormitory, which happened to be in the main School hall however I was quite surprised by the absence of any beds. The floor was strewn with straw filled mattresses, which she referred to as palliasse's, for us to sleep on. My initial thoughts were that they looked very "ethnic". More like something that the Lone Ranger or Hopalong would have slept upon, not a kiddy in Devon. After supper we did our nightly ablutions and we Small Eggs turned in for the night.

I was surprised just how comfortable the mattress "thingamajig" was however I suppose that by the time we were told to go to bed we were all so tired that we would have slept anywhere.

I don't think that I had ever felt as content before as there was so much to look forward to. Bray Wood School and life back at New Lodge now seemed like a distant memory. At the back of my mind. However I had two nagging concerns. One of the ladies wished us all goodnight and she then said "Sleep tight and don't let the bed bugs bite". Although I had heard the expression before, and even used it myself, I still wasn't too sure what a bed bug was or what one might have looked like. I kept thinking of my own bed, back at Windsor, with its lovely thick mattress, and then of all the stuffing in my mattress here and that it might be full of all sorts of nasties. Francis said that it was a saying that old ladies like to tell to children however I decided that I wouldn't take any chances and pulled my jim-jams into my socks, just for safety.

The second concern was Peter the tortoise. John and George had stopped talking about him and, frankly, I had completely forgotten about him. I reminded myself to speak to John about Peter over breakfast the next day. With these concerns now resolved I quickly fell into a deep sleep.

The next morning we were woken extra early when the Church bells, next door, began to chime. Over breakfast I confronted George and John about Peter the Tortoise. I'm afraid the news was not what I wanted to hear. According to George, when he went down to see Peter the tortoise in his "run" in the garden at New Lodge, just before we left for our holiday, he was nowhere to be seen. He had, effectively, vanished from the face of the earth.

As he could see that I was getting very distressed by this news he "upped it a little to make it sound better. I think that they call this positive spin! "Actually," said George, "I think that Peter is now living a happy life in Windsor Great Park". "Look Tubs," he continued "it was really no life for a tortoise cooped up here in a home with a load of maladjusted children. He's much better off on his own".

"Well, if you put it that way he probably is better off," I replied and "by the way, are we all maladjusted or is it just the Large Eggs like you that are weird?" George looked to the skies and mumbled something very rude under his breath.

We departed in good time for the beach and by the time we reached it was still relatively empty. In fact we were so early that there was still a sea-mist blowing onto the beach. It was a spectacular sight and all I could hear were the waves lapping onto the rocks. As we made our way to the breakwater beach we caught our first glimpse of the harbour (below). We youngsters all thought it was very pretty sight in fact it was just how we might have imagined an old fashioned British seaside port to be.

I was really taken back by the sight of all the ships in the harbour. At school we had recently been learning about the Spanish Armada and the ships of that time and I began to wonder whether any of the ships in the harbour went back that far. I remember that the town was very hilly and built around the harbour which was still an active dock for fishing trawlers. As we all stood there, looking out at the bay, we could see the trawlers coming in and out of the harbour, followed by flocks of noisy seagulls. What was really interesting was that when one turned around the view was completely different. The harbour had lots of old boats and we were all really keen to explore them.

At some point during the morning we were introduced to a very old man that our master referred to as an "old sea dog" who was to tell us something about the history of the harbour and the fishing industry.

We were told that the term 'sea dog' referred to a very, very old man who had spent all of his time at sea. I couldn't stop staring at him because his hair was as white as snow and he was growing it from every available orifice in his head. I wondered how he did that as I didn't have any except upon the top of my head. I came to the conclusion that it grew like that to keep him warm at sea.

He told us that in 1944 Brixham played a significant role in the D-Day landings when British warships, and part of the D-Day fleet, had sailed out from there. Also, for centuries, ships sailing in the English Channel would come into the local bays to seek refuge from the storms and to replenish food supplies. He also told us about HMS Vanguard, which was in the harbour, a British battleship built during the WW11. According to the hairy old sea-dog she was the biggest and fastest of the Royal Navy's battleships and the world's last ship of its kind to be built. Apparently she was scheduled to convey King George VI and his family on the first Royal Tour of South Africa which was cancelled as a result of to King George's declining health. Vanguard briefly became flagship of the Mediterranean Fleet in early 1949 and in 1952-3 was to participate in the Queen's Coronation Review. This was all very exciting and the older boys expressed their wish to go to the harbour and see the ship for themselves.

Over the coming days of our holiday a routine was soon established: an early morning hike to the beach, playtime in the morning with a packed lunch and then either more beach playing, a walk or an excursion. Some of the older boys were allowed to wander off by themselves. John came back one day to say that they had all been swimming off of the breakwater beach when some of the local lads began to chant and sneer at them. Although he didn't elaborate to the master he later told us that they challenged the lads to a stone skimming contest. It seems that our lads did themselves proud and made some new local friends in the process. One morning, as we were all marching down to the beach, one of the boys started to whistle that tune that I had heard when we arrived the previous week. Suddenly some of them broke out into song, called 'Down Windsor Way' (music page iii).

> *There is a mouldy dump*
> *Down Windsor Way*
> *Where we get bread and cheese*
> *Three times a day*
> *Eggs and bacon*
> *We don't see*
> *We get sawdust in our tea*
> *We are gradually*
> *Fading away, fading away, fading away!*

As we passed people they were all looking at us and applauding the singing. According to George it was the traditional song of New Lodge and it was called "Down Windsor Way". Apparently Sir didn't like the song, as it gave a false message and he certainly did not want us to sing it in public. He reckoned that the words failed to recognise the great achievements of our Benefactor and what he had done for the likes of destitute children like us. Well we didn't quite see things in that light. John reckoned that we were the innocent ones who found themselves in this situation and it was adults that need to be taught to be upright citizens and consider a more regimented life.

As the singing stopped nurse came rushing to the front of the marching line and accused us all of being "Ungrateful little brats. That there are children in the East End of London who have never seen the sea or had a holiday". One of the Large Eggs whispered loudly, so that most of us could hear, "Yes, and some of us are from the East End and this is our first time as well and it's not our fault". Nurse was livid with us and kept tight-lipped for the rest of the morning.

A day or two before we were scheduled to return to Windsor it was decided that all of the children would enjoy their final holiday excursion aboard a paddle steamer trip around Torbay. Some of us had already seen the paddle steamer sailing in the distance, earlier in the week.

I wondered what all the fuss was about as it looked historic, just like the type of boat that I had seen and read about in one of our comics. Anyway by the time we arrived at the quayside there was a mad scramble to locate and sit on the best seats on the boat. I thought that the best place was on the highest part of the deck and that is where I made for. According to the souvenir brochure we were going to enjoy a nostalgic cruise around the beautiful bay where the sounds and smells will transport you back in time to an era when ships were the life blood of the community. This paddle steamer was one of the last remaining coal-fired paddle steamers in operation in the UK and her engines were even older than the boat itself, dating back to 1904, and eight years before the Titanic sank.

I don't know whether it was the sight of the old wooden hulks in the main harbour or the excitement of being out on the sea, with the wind blowing in my hair, but my thoughts suddenly took me back to old Tyke, the smuggler-cum-pirate I knew from Yearnor Woods. In particular I remembered the excitement I felt as I lay in wait for him to turn up at Ashley Coombe. I remember thinking that I liked life by the seaside and that being on board a ship had an unexpected excitement for me. I hadn't felt quite as pleased with myself and my situation since I first donned my army uniform and yearned to enlist in the army. As we chugged around the harbour I felt a level of contentment and satisfaction never felt before. To me things couldn't get any better than this. I was very surprised by my reaction and began to wonder whether life at sea might be the best thing for me once I had become an adult.

Only time would tell!

In the meantime several of the boys were now beginning to feel very queasy, in spite of the sea being as calm as a mill pond. A couple of the older boys decided to make fun out of their plight but they were swiftly reprimanded by the nurse who told them "that the worst thing that you can do for anybody that is seasick is to make any mention of food or drink". As she finished telling us about what one should or shouldn't do or say to somebody feeling seasick several of the lads suddenly turned even greener. One bright spark told them that the boy that looked the most seasick, before we hit dry land for a cream tea, would be rewarded with a lovely smelly kipper.

I wonder whether they ever found their sea legs!

The boat trip aboard the paddle steamer marked the concluding stage of our holiday and our final days were spent on the beach. Overall I think that we had been very good and had behaved impeccably, a real credit to our Benefactor. Apart from one or two incidents I do not think that Sir would have had anything to complain about us.

The train ride home was relatively uneventful and I had a sudden realisation that the excitement we felt two weeks before could not be recreated on the return journey home. Despite travelling behind a lovely old steam train I could not resurrect those feelings of anticipation that I felt previously. This journey was to take us all back to the realism of school, the New Lodge routine and being cautious about who you spoke to and what you said to them. If that wasn't enough there was also the prospect that "warm legs Sonny Jim" might soon become reactivated after his summer holidays.

A reunion, the Coronation, we meet Martin & a visit to London Airport

Shortly after our return from holiday John received information that our mother had been in touch with Family Advisory. Apparently she wished to re-establish regular contact with her sons now that they were living closer to London. John did suggest, to the rest of us, that our moving to New Lodge was to encourage our mother to visit us on a more regular basis and that in the future we might be repatriated to her. I felt inclined to tell John of my indignation over such a suggestion. After all, it was our parent's that put us in the care of Barnardo's in the first place. Also, over the past six or so years she had hardly been in contact with us. I could see that John was in an awkward position because, as he was now thirteen years of age, he was much more aware of all the toing and froing that was going on between our mother and Barnardo's.

Anyway we were told that she was coming to visit us, on her own, on the following Sunday afternoon for tea, and that we needed to be ready and dressed in our Sunday best by 11.00 am precisely. Well, we waited in the playroom until lunchtime and she had not turned up. The nurse told us to change back into our "indoor" clothes, have lunch, change back again into Sunday best and reconvene in the playroom at 1.00 pm. We met again at the agreed hour and she eventually turned up at 2.30 pm in the afternoon. I have to say that any warm feelings I had for my mother were quickly dispelled by her late arrival. We had spent all of lives parading, marching, getting up, going to bed and even eating to a bell and she couldn't even turn up to see us on time. Francis and I could not understand how she could treat us this way. Did we, in any way, actually mean anything to her at all?

Anyway she made her apologies, about the traffic in Windsor, and said that now she knew the route she would be punctual for her next visit. It was a warm autumn afternoon and she asked if we would join her for a walk.

She had, however, an ulterior motive for getting us away from the main building! As we walked away from the confines of New Lodge, down the road towards the woods, I experienced a feeling of déjà vu. Standing by a van, parked by the entrance to a field, was a man who seemed strangely familiar to me. Neither John nor George recognised him and so I assumed that he wasn't Tenby.

Then the penny dropped.

I whispered to Francis that that bloke by the van was none other than the dentist from Ashley Coombe. As we got closer to him my mother said "Now boys, I would like you to meet your Uncle Bill. We are hoping that over the next few months we will all get to know each other well".

Well, we all politely offered him our hands to shake and each of us said to him "Good afternoon Sir". John told our mother that we had not sought permission to leave the grounds of New Lodge and that if we didn't get back soon we might all be in trouble with Sir. As a result our visit was cut short, and as Uncle Bill returned to the van to wait for her, we went with our mother back to the dining room for tea.

On our way back I remember feeling baffled about this experience and that I had some questions for her that I wanted to get off my chest. She tended to avoid them and I came to the conclusion that she regarded my questioning of her as a bit of a liberty. I guess that there were a lot of them and so I couldn't really blame her. I was particularly confused as to how Uncle Bill could be my uncle when I didn't know his wife who would have been my auntie? I would say that my meeting with her left me in a confused state of mind and I made my feelings known to my brothers.

At least in New Lodge the days were very predictable as we knew what to expect on a day to day basis, but that afternoon I felt uncertain, anxious and what's more she had broken the rules about leaving the grounds of New Lodge without permission!

A couple of weeks later we were, again, informed that she was to make another visit on the Sunday at noon. The same thing happened; we changed for lunch, changed back into best clothes and then waited all afternoon for her arrival. She failed to turn up. Whether there was a genuine reason for the failure to attend we were never informed. Over the next month or two our mother's visits continued but she was never punctual and we were kept waiting for her, but at least she showed up and I was beginning to warm to her again. Uncle Bill didn't make another appearance until just before we were repatriated back together again. This final visit must have been regarded as extra special by Barnardo's. We were informed by the nurse that Uncle Bill would be present in his official capacity, whatever that meant, and that he would be taking us all to London Airport for the day and we would be meeting our half-brother, Martin, for the first time.

Well! Now you are talking, airports and planes were fantastic but Martin who?

Although, for us boys, the jury was still out about our mother and our feelings for her I did find Uncle Bill to be quite affable. To be truthful we hadn't had too much time to get to know him and I had my concerns over his function within the new emerging family. Was he a real relative of mine and what was to be his role in our future lives together? These were the questions that I really needed answers to and I had to make all of my enquiries through John who probably told me what he thought I should hear! As far as I was concerned, at that precise time, my relationship with Lugwig or old Mr. Macey was stronger than the one I had with our mother or Uncle Bill. When you think about it, for the past six and a half years she had played no part in my life, and up until then it was just John, George and Francis. Now things were changing and I was suddenly being told to accept a couple of unknown "outsiders" into my life, and accept them as my parents. I was uncertain how I should do this and how it might affect me.

By June 1953 everybody was talking about the Queen's forthcoming Coronation. The boys in New Lodge were as excited as the next man, about the forthcoming celebrations, even though they were unlikely to impact upon us personally. The coronation of Queen Elizabeth II took place on 2 June 1953 at Westminster Abbey in London following the death of her father, King George VI, on 6 February 1952. Most of the boys were taken, by coach, to Windsor to enjoy the celebrations there but I was considered to be too young and the staff were concerned for my safety what with all the crowds of people expected to be by the Castle. As an extra special treat I was allowed to watch the service on a black and white television in the Gardener's Lodge of our home. I was intrigued by the contraption as the cabinet, that held the TV, was enormous and the screen really small. The main problem was that the picture wasn't static it kept flicking upwards and my host didn't really know how to deal with it apart from adjusting the aerial. Anyway I hadn't seen anything like it before and kept asking him loads of questions which the poor man seemed to be unable to answer but really I think that I was being a nuisance and he just wanted to enjoy the spectacle in peace!. It was all so mysterious to me but I was pleased to have seen the event.

At school, on the Monday following the Coronation, the celebrations continued and all of the children were given some commemorative gifts. I was given a special glass Coronation mug with a certificate as well as a manual of photographs of the Royal Family and of the Coronation itself.

This was followed by a special party of celebration at my school. I made a bee-line for my German friend Anthony during the party. As a foreigner I was keen to see how he felt about our Royal Family. The Queen and her family were the only real family that I was familiar with, and so over the years she became part of my family. I remember feeling quite disappointed by Anthony's response because although he loved the gifts he said that "he didn't really know who she was and that he certainly didn't have strong feelings for her or for her family. Why should he?" To Anthony she was just a nice lady and that this was a nice day and the pageantry was, well, just nice.

It was as Anthony was talking about his feelings for the Queen that I realised that this was how I felt about our mother. She seemed a nice lady who did some nice things for me. In reality, however, I had a stronger tie to the Queen; after all, she and had been with me through thick and thin and she was the only true family that I had ever known. It was she who was the last person I saw and spoke to, every night, before I went to sleep. As those celebrations subsided another great excitement loomed on the horizon.

At last the day arrived when we were all going to London Airport with our mother. On this occasion she was punctual and we left New Lodge in haste as we had lots to do and much ground to cover. Shortly after we left the perimeter of the grounds of the lodge we could all see Uncle Bill standing next to his van with a young lad by his side.

As we approached them our mother said "Right boys, I would like you to meet your youngest brother Martin".

"Hello Martin, it is very nice to meet you" we replied and we shook his hand and then all piled into the van.

"Next stop London Airport" said Uncle Bill.

I was particularly pleased when I discovered that Martin was, in fact, younger than me. This meant that the first time I would have seniority over somebody in my family just like John and George did with Francis and me! I was thinking to myself how great it was going to be having a younger brother looking up to me for a change and that I might lord it over him. Then I realised, in fact, that Martin was not that much shorter than me and had a similar build. He was not going to be a pushover after all. Martin mentioned to me in the van just how much he was looking forward to having his brothers living at home with him and to protect him from any bullies but most of all he was longing to be reunited with Peter, his pet and much missed tortoise. I decided that as far as Peter was concerned I was going to "be like dad and keep mum" about him for the time being. We kept the conversation quite clipped, although there were oodles to talk about, sitting in the back of this smelly old van was not conducive to lively conversation. I did tell Martin about our trip to Hooton Aerodrome and that we had been given access to walk all over a bomber and he told me that he had a collection of cuttings of aircrafts for me to look at when we came home to Walthamstow.

Martin and I "hit it off from the start" and I liked him a lot and although we had only been together that day for a short time I felt close to him. My relationship with Martin was like no other that I had with John, George or Francis. I wasn't able to put my finger on precisely what it was or why, but I felt different with him. I guess the idea of having a family member that was younger than myself was the hope that I had always sought. I could look after a younger sibling, like I did with teddy, and tell other lads to "Leave him alone he is my "bruv" and you will have to contend with me first"!

As we approached the airport we were directed into a fenced off area, adjacent to one of the runways, and we were able to picnic and watch the planes "taking off and landing" to our hearts desire. At the earliest convenient moment our mother took a picture of us both with Martin (on the left) and myself saying "hello" for the first time. In the picture I am dressed in my official "outdoor" Barnardo clothing which contrasts with Martin's more casual look.

It seems inconceivable, today, but in 1953 we were allowed easy access to the airport. In those days commercial air travel was in its infancy and, on cost alone, it tended to be limited to royalty and the wealthy. It was amazing that we were able to watch the aircraft landing and taking off from the fenced off areas adjacent to the runways. We were all mesmerised by the aircraft that we saw on our visit. In particular I was impressed by their size and the fact that they didn't seem to be flying particularly fast.

BOAC Comet

Boeing 377 Stratocruiser

Lockheed Constellation

How did they manage to stay up there in the sky without tumbling down? I remember Martin telling me that this was a day to remember as he had never seen so many planes, at close quarters, and just how shiny their aluminium fuselage were against the fabulous blue sky. "Oh, and something else," said Martin, "it was great to meet you all at last".

After the excitement of the planes we sat down on the grass for a picnic lunch and, as usual, I was starving. Our faces lit up at the selection of goodies for us to nosh up and pronto. For us boys this couldn't get any better; aircraft, food and a new brother into the bargain.

Our mother continued to photograph us with box camera and this photograph (below), of her with Uncle Bill, was taken by Francis at the airport and has always been a favourite.

I suppose our mother realised that with seven people in the back of a van the journey home would not be a good time to update us with her plans for the future, and so before we left London Airport she decided to give us an update. She told us of her meetings with the Barnardo's Family group and that they were as keen as she was for us to be repatriated into her care. She told us that she had never intended for us to be institutionalised for such a long time and that her plans had been thwarted on many fronts. Anyway, she anticipated that we would be living as a family together in Walthamstow, East London, within the next twelve months.

The times they are a changing!!

Santa pays a visit

As we approached our first Christmas at New Lodge there was again a sense of anticipation in the air. We were told that every year there was a tradition for the boys from New Lodge, and other local children homes, to be entertained by soldiers from Victoria Barracks close to Windsor Castle.

He went on tell us that these were the Queen's elite Corp of soldiers, the very troops that set off daily to change the guard at Windsor Castle.

For me this was one of the most exciting events of the year and I asked the master if I could return to the dorm for a minute as I had left something behind. Actually I had only one thing on my mind. I was convinced that, although Sir had banned me from wearing my army uniform it would be OK for me to wear it when we went to the barracks. I rushed upstairs and retrieved it from the place where it had been hidden, from view, for the past few months, under my mattress.

To my horror I could no longer get into the trousers as they were too tight, the blouson too small and only the beret fitted. I remember thinking that I would look pretty daft just wearing the beret and so I abandoned the idea. As I left the dorm I was feeling really crestfallen that the uniform, my pride and joy, no longer fitted me and that it was now redundant. The master asked me, "If I found what I was looking for".

"No," I replied. "I thought I knew exactly where it was Sir, but it wasn't there."

"Oh well let's get on then. We've a party to go to," he replied.

Shortly afterwards a military lorry drew up outside the front entrance, and we all tumbled into the back. It was such fun and I felt like a real soldier standing there next to some regulars. I kept pointing to bits of their kit and uniform and asking them all about it. I was in my element.

Eventually we arrived at the camp and were immediately ushered into what looked like a theatre. We were each given a glass of orange and then the show began. The soldiers put on a pantomime for us. It was so funny and every time we shouted out "He's behind you" the character would say "No he isn't, you naughty boys and girls," and then he would get himself into all kinds of mischief.

After the panto we were given a song-sheet and then we had a sing song. I remember singing Christmas carols including the one about "Washing my Socks by Night"-Tee Hee Hee! When we began singing a song about "My old man said follow the van" I suddenly thought about our mother, Uncle Bill and Martin and wished that they were here with me to enjoy all the jolly japes. Suddenly and unexpectedly Father Christmas appeared form nowhere. I was absolutely dumbstruck! I had never met him before in my life and I was spellbound by the redness of his outfit. We had an enjoyable pantomime style entertainment with Santa and just before the end we were all given a present wrapped up in shiny paper.

My present was a detective set consisting of a spy glass, invisible ink, just in case I need to write a secret letter, and a false moustache for disguise. I loved my gift and this was a magical afternoon. After the fun had stopped we had tea together and then returned back to New Lodge.

We had only been travelling for a few minutes when the lorry came to an abrupt halt. It was quite dark and getting chilly and from the back of the lorry we could hear the soldiers trying to see what was wrong. One of the soldiers came to the back of the lorry and asked whether any of us had a torch.

I immediately said "Yes I have a torch. It's my prized possession and it looks like Pluto. I call it my Pluto torch," I replied.

He then asked "if it would be possible to borrow my Pluto torch".

I said that "I didn't mind provided he took good care of it as it was very precious".

"Well" he said "where is it then Sonny?"

"Oh it isn't here, I haven't got it with me it's in my locker back at New Lodge. I thought you were just asking us a question out of interest. Sorry," I said.

I think he was upset because he went away shaking his head from side to side and using words that I had only ever heard the Large Eggs using. Eventually the soldiers managed to get the lorry started up again and we were soon back at New Lodge. I asked the soldier whether he would like to see my pluto torch. He told me that he had a better offer and declined.

I couldn't think of anything that might take priority over a "pluto" torch. I obviously had a lot of growing up to do and as New Year (1954) was beckoning I knew that we were in for some great changes ahead of us!

CHAPTER FOUR

More visits and social relatives

As we entered the New Year, 1954, there were definite indicators that our time at New Lodge may be coming to an end. Firstly our mother was making more frequent visits, mostly unaccompanied, and on occasions she would take us all out for the day.

During one visit she bought her best friend Doreen to meet us. I remember her as being very pleasant and they were both dressed like film starlets. Although I had never actually seen a film at the cinema our mother would bring some of Martin's comics for us and I remember seeing pictures of Hollywood actresses in one of them. To me she looked and dressed up like one of them. On this occasion she was wearing what looked to me like a jacket made out of rat or mouse fur. She said that it was called "faux" fur and that the collar was actually made of real fur. Overall I thought she looked very pretty.

As well as visits from our Mother it was also suggested that Francis and I should become socialised, in preparation for our future repatriation, with the help of what were termed 'social relatives'. These were volunteer adults who were caring enough to provide 'institutionalised' children with a more family-oriented lifestyle compared to Barnardo's.

In time we were introduced to Auntie Phyllis and her husband. Unfortunately neither Francis nor I ever knew his name and so we never called him anything. One Saturday morning a large limousine drew up outside and Auntie Phyllis and her husband came out to greet us. We were told, by Sir, that we would be going to stay with them for the weekend and our overnight bags had been already packed for us. We got into the back of their car and drove to their home in Eton. It seemed very big for an "outsider" home and it had a large garden in the front and at the back. I must say they went out of their way to make us feel very welcome.

They introduced us to their son, Alex, who seemed to be about my age but much better dressed in a very nice suit and tie. We introduced ourselves to him but he didn't seem to be in the slightest bit interested in us or even willing to play with us. He appeared to be sulky and petulant and unwilling to really speak with us or join in the occasion. I guess that I would have felt the same if a couple of strange interlopers were suddenly imposed on me.

My initial response to him and his attitude towards us is that he might have benefitted from a knuckle sandwich as that usually did the trick back home. However Francis said that as we were on test, to see if we could go home, so we had better be well behaved.

It was a shame that we had come empty-handed and had nothing that we could offer Alex in the way of a gift which may have broken the ice. Unfortunately we literally had little in the way of personal possessions at New Lodge. Auntie Phyllis, sensing that all was not going too well, invited us to play together in Alex's playroom.

When we saw the plethora of toys there we just couldn't believe our eyes. He had just about everything that a little boy would want displayed like a Gamage's Christmas catalogue. Well, we both had a great time playing whereas Alex looked on with a troubled expression on his face as though he had lost a shilling and found a farthing. Unfortunately over the coming weeks we found it increasingly difficult to engage with Alex at all and inevitably this was to impact our time with the family. Over the coming few months we visited Auntie Phyllis on several occasions, sometimes with Francis, and other times on my own. Our relationship with Alex, however, never improved and eventually our visits stopped altogether.

Nevertheless Auntie Phyllis continued to write to us both and to send us cards for our birthdays and the nurse helped me to compose little notes back to her. Yes, you could say that we had both become quite attached to her and her husband but we could not get Alex to open up to us. It's a shame really and to this day I still believe that the knuckle sandwich might just have done the trick for us.

We are acclimatised, we are on our way.

Shortly afterwards we happen to mention our visit to Eton to John and George and they suggested that they were what was officially called 'acclimatisation visits'. These were visits made to "outsiders" and their homes in preparation for the final reunion with our mother. I asked them what they meant exactly by that and they reckoned that living in New Lodge was very different to life on the "outside" and that staying with auntie Phyllis, in her big house, was much more like the real thing. The experience that we had gained would help to prepare us for our new life on the 'outside'.

I asked John whether he thought we really needed to become 'outsiders' at all and he told me that we couldn't stay in care for ever. He told us that Barnardo's only had responsibility for us until we were fifteen and as he and George were getting on in years, and the authorities didn't want to split us up, then we would all have to leave together. Well, we soon discovered that John's hypothesis about preparing us for life 'outside' and the big houses there were 'outside' New Lodge could not have been further from the truth.

I wasn't really sure where John got all of his information from but he continued to remind us, almost on a daily basis, that we wold soon be returning home. He maintained this mantra for many weeks despite us remaining in New Lodge.

Somehow, however, his rhetoric began to percolate through me and one morning, completely unawares as the teacher went on and on irritating me, I suddenly blurted out to that I couldn't wait to leave and return home to my mother in London.

Well I guess that was the first he had heard about me leaving and during the break I suspect that he spoke to the Headmaster who asked to see me later on in the day.

"Now William, I hear from your teacher that you will soon be leaving us. Is that true?" said Sir.

"Yes Sir, well as far as I know." I replied.

"What do you mean William? Are you leaving us or not?" said Sir.

I replied "That I was, but it was up to mother to come and take us". Anyway he would be told about any changes in our circumstances in due course.

The next thing I knew one of the masters at New Lodge told me to stop spreading rumours or I'd be in trouble. I informed him that as far as John knew we were all in the process of being acclimatised for our return to our mother. It became clear to me that he knew nothing about this either. He called me a bloody little fool and that I needed to stop exaggerating or I would soon be in big trouble.

I returned to John and asked him just how certain he was about our forthcoming move and he replied that it was imminent, or even sooner, depending upon our mother. I was still in the dark and decided to say no more about it until the car was outside the door and Sir was preparing to wave us off.

Then with little warning, one Sunday afternoon in Mid-August of 1954, our mother suddenly turned up with Uncle Bill and Martin in their van. Our mother told us that we were going home that very day and that we needed to pack our possessions for the last time. I had very little in the way of possessions apart from the clothes that I was wearing, which Sir said we must take with us, my 'Pluto' torch, my souvenir brochure of the Queen's Coronation and my blue mug. That was it.

My own personal goodbyes

I sat on my bed and took a final look around my dorm. As I thought about teddy and Wolly and wondering what had become of them I realised that Ashley Coombe was, now, just a distant memory. That my life had changed a lot over the past years and that it was now going to change yet again. That this, the first part of my life, was now coming to an end and that my brothers and I now had the next stage to look forward to along with Martin.

Inexplicably I began to shed a few tears over the highs and lows of my life in Barnardo's and now my comfort blanket was now disappearing. I suddenly became aware that it was all up to me from now on. I was to make my own decisions, choose what to wear and what to eat and eventually how to make the most of my life. That however comes a little later on.

In the meantime was I just daydreaming and kidding myself again?

The staff were all assembled and waiting on the steps of New Lodge when we finally emerged for the last time. We said our 'goodbyes' and our 'please keep in touch' and please 'write soon won't you' to the other boys. I thought of Anthony and how the life-changes that I was experiencing now were nothing compared to his. I was missing my old German mate already!! Then we all piled into Uncle Bill's van and headed east!

I remember the moment well and as I looked back through the rear window I saw the masters and some of the boys waving frantically at us. Then as I cast my eyes upwards towards my bedroom window there was teddy. He looked sad as he gazed out of the window at me waving goodbye to me for the very last time.

I also felt sad and waved back at him. Then they were all gone.

We were now the 'outsiders'. I now felt different and even though Martin was with me I felt sad and at a loss. The back of the van was certainly not a place where one should try to feel sorry for oneself; it was actually blinking uncomfortable with just a couple of wooden boxes to sit, on by the wheel arches. However we were now heading into a new life and a new adventure together with our mother and my new brother.

As I sat quietly reminiscing about what had just happened to us I wondered why Uncle Bill had come in this contraption and not the smart limousine like the one that Auntie Phyllis had driven me around in. After all, according to John, 'outsiders' lived in better places than we were used to. That's why we were now completely acclimatised to their new way of life and I couldn't wait to see what kind of mansion we would be living in once we reached Walthamstow in East London.

Suddenly all of my sadness and ill-feelings came to an abrupt end when Uncle Bill declared "Who's for fish and chips then".

"Yeeeeeah" we all replied

It was dark when we arrived for the first time in our new home and so our inspection of the property would have to wait until daybreak and the sound of the new bugle boy. But who will be around to perform it?

CHAPTER FIVE

Introduction - a new life and a new home,
but does it measure up?

The first night that we spent in our new home in Boston Road, in August 1954, has remained indelibly imprinted upon my memory for a number of reasons.

For a start this was the first night ever that I had slept anywhere, other than in a dormitory of an approved official bone fide Barnardo home, apart from the weekends spent at Auntie Phyllis's.

Also I wasn't too sure that I liked sleeping in a bed with somebody else's coat on the top to keep me warm. I kept thinking about the 'bed bugs biting' when we went to Brixham and how that made me feel itchy. Also, although Martin was in my room, I wanted Francis as well just like it had been over the previous eight years.

You could say that the events of the day had taken their toll, and although I felt both physically and mentally exhausted I was still unable to nod off as quickly as I usually did. I started to think of the things that I wanted to do as Martin had already promised to show us around his manor. I was particularly excited by this prospect as he had already seen the extent of our manor at New Lodge, and I wanted to see the extent of our mothers land and house to see how it measured up. I also thought that I should write a letter to Anthony, to explain that I wasn't returning to Bray Wood School, and that I would like to keep in touch with him, as well as another note to Auntie Phyllis to tell her that I had arrived safely in my new home in Walthamstow. Just before I actually dozed off I remember wondering who would sound the bugle to let us know that breakfast was ready and that, at 6.30 am, it was time to get up. Little did I know then that I had an awful lot of learning and growing-up to do and that I needed to do this very, very quickly!

Where's our house?
Around our manor and the roller skate incident

The next morning I awoke fairly early, as was the norm at New Lodge, but I was surprised not to hear a bugle call to rally us round. With a sense of anticipation I looked out of the bedroom window and cast my eye over the estate that was now our new home (below). Crikey, I thought, it's enormous and much bigger than I thought it would be. Each house had a bay and these were each about the size of the Gardener's cottage back at New Lodge and they housed just two people. I guessed that we must have four of these bays. After all we had a family of seven!

But where were the parkland and the lawns?

I woke Martin and asked him "Who was supposed to blow the bugle in the morning?"

He said "that now I was in London there would be no more bugle calls unless I wanted to go onto the roof and wake the neighbourhood up myself."

"What neighbourhood do you mean Mart?" I asked.

He said to me "Look Tubs who do you think you are Lord Snooty. This is the East end of London not Windsor. You need to get a reality check."

"Is Lord Snooty one of our neighbour's then Mart?" I enquired

Martin looked at me and said "Billy, you are no longer in the homes and so you need to think like a Walthamstow lad. There are no Lords and Ladies around here, no big mansions and manors and certainly no blinking buglers to wake us up every morning. Today I am going to take you to look around your new manor".

"So we do have a manor that we live in, Mart?" I asked.

"Billy just shut up asking me questions and I'll show you what kind of manor you are living in, OK" replied Martin.

"OK Martin but just answer me this: how many of the houses out there in the road are ours? Is it three or four? I guessed three but it might be four" I asked

"Billy, what planet have you been living on? This is it! This is 23 Boston Road E17. It is just this one house. It's this house and nobody else's house. We do not live next door because somebody else lives in that one, and we don't live in the house next to that one because somebody else lives in that one. Do you get the picture now?" he said.

"Oh Martin," I sighed "What about all the acclimatisation to prepare us ready for living as 'outsiders'. Are you telling me that this is it?"

Martin looked heavenward and nodded approvingly.

When I arrived in the kitchen John, George and Francis were already sitting at the table waiting for breakfast to be served or to serve themselves. We spoke together about the size of the house and that we were all going to have to now share and that we had no gardens to play in; only the street. Martin came in and asked us what we wanted for breakfast.

I said "Just porridge, toast and a cup of tea".

He told us that we could have anything we wanted for breakfast provided that we helped ourselves and prepared it.

Hopefully our mother's done the shopping and there's some food in the cupboard".

I was taken aback by this as we had never had to prepare our own breakfast before.

"Isn't our mother or somebody going to prepare breakfast for us?" asked George to which Martin made a comment along the lines that if preparing our own breakfast that wasn't good enough for us toffee-nosed Lord Snootys then we needed to get off of our high horses and get a reality check.

I found some cereal and milk and we all had our first breakfast together and a foretaste of our future lives-Boston Road style!

After breakfast we decided to take Martin up on his offer to show us around the local area. What he termed his manor. It was through talking to Martin that I realised that his notion of estate and manors was not in the same context as we were used to from our experiences at Ashley Coombe, Marfords or New Lodge. In fact it was diametrically opposite. When Martin spoke of "estates" he was referring to the local council estates and not the farming and country estates that we had grown up in. We also found out that Martin's notion of a manor had nothing to do with large country houses with horses and hounds and more to do with the territories that the local street urchins regarded as theirs, and that they were ready to protect from any infiltrators.

As we left our house, in Boston Road, Martin gave us some general directions in case one of us became lost. George had arranged with Martin, beforehand, to borrow his skates and roller skate along with us as we explored the local area together. I became aware of a complete absence of countryside. It was road after road after road with hundreds of houses and very little open space. It was such a contrast to the places that we were used to. I also noticed was that on occasions as we walked through particular built up areas some of the local lads would hang around 'sussing us up'. Martin told us not to say anything as we would soon be off their patch. He did mention that some of his school friends lived along that particular road and had a 'tasty way of dealing with lippy yobbos'. I didn't ask him to elaborate as his colourful description spoke for itself.

We hadn't walked far when suddenly a group of similar aged lads started to cat-call and heckle us. It reminded me of a gang stand-off in a western. Unfortunately one of the lads misjudged us completely, especially George. I guess that being the tallest of all of us George did look a bit gawky and the roller skates would not have shown him off in the best light. In hindsight, however, the hecklers had probably picked upon the wrong bunch of urchins as we were able to stick up and defend ourselves with no trouble at all. It was George who demonstrated this so admirably.

It was a moment of sheer lunacy and poor decision-making when one of the lads directed his detrimental comments specifically towards George. In particular he thought that George looked like a right 'tart' in his girly roller skates. Now George was always the silent one, a 'deadly assassin', and able to stand his ground against any would be assailant. We all stood in amazement as he roller-skated over to the lad removed one of the skates and sloshed him around his chops with it. He laced the skate back on to his foot and skated back to us. When I looked back the group of lads had disappeared with only the residue dust and 'tumble weed' remaining and blowing in the wind.

I guess that at one time we might have called that justice Barnardo-style but now it was really justice Walthamstow-style!

We wandered back to Boston Road to see what our mother had prepared for our lunch. One of the earliest observations that I made, now that we were 'outsiders', was that life here was never going to be like the one that we had been used to. The routine of institutional life does have its benefits with very regular food, clean clothes and minimal chores. We all found our mother to be a disorganised person, and food and its preparation seemed to be quite low on her list of priorities. On arrival nothing hot was prepared and so we just made ourselves a sandwich and decided that in the afternoon Martin would show us one of the local green spaces, 'Queens Road Park, and we could have a kick-about with the football.

A football match, Tubs gets lost and Beaky's trike!

It was good to see some green open space again, for the first time in a while, and we couldn't wait to rush about and release some of our energy and pent-up anxieties. Yes, despite the uncertainties about leaving care and now being in a permanent family home to me, and I sensed some of the others, there was still an element of cautiousness about our day to day situation in Walthamstow. Anyway it was time for a bit of footie, not my favourite of past-times, but still it was good to be out in the open air again.

"Pass me the ball, Blamp," I said to Francis but instead he passed it to George who in turn kicked it to Beaky (Martin). Now, out of Barnardo's it made more sense to us to address each other by our nicknames. I was never really quite sure why we made that decision. I was known as Tubs, Martin was Beaky, Francis was Blamp, George was Slugs and John, well he was just John.

Anyway I was getting really fed up with them because they were ignoring me and my requests for a shot at the ball. I was becoming increasingly urdy as they kept kicking it backwards and forwards to each other and snubbing me completely. As I wasn't getting my own way, I did what I always did well and I took myself off in a sulk and I left the park. Unfortunately the others were so interested in their game that they failed to notice that I had gone, and by the time they had noticed I must have been well and truly out of sight. I had no idea where I was or in which direction I should take to get back to Boston Road.

I was well and truly lost.

The main problem was that every street looked the same, rows upon rows of terraced houses with bay windows and a pub or a shop on each corner. "What if I am never able to find my way back home again", I wondered, and the thought made me start to cry aloud. I hadn't been crying for that long when a couple of kind ladies pushing prams came up and asked me what was wrong. I blurted out the address and telephone number that our mother had made me memorise and they said that they would take me home, which they kindly did.

Upon arrival the others asked me why I had disappeared on my own as they had gone looking for me. I told them that they were beastly and nasty and that I was never going to speak to them ever again. I went to my bedroom and about an hour later, after I had calmed down and stopped holding my breath in protest, I went downstairs and asked them where they were going to take me the next day.

As it happens I went out with Beaky to the park again, just the two of us this time, and with him he brought his pride and joy, a three-wheeled tricycle. Beaky was proudly riding his bike up and down a gradient in the park and getting more and more excited as he started to feel the effect of the bike accelerating on the downward part of his journey. It was then that I suggested that I might be able to increase his fun further with a little push from yours truly. With Beaky's agreement we tried a few pushes but he kept asking me to push harder and faster, which, of course, I was only too pleased to oblige. Unfortunately for Beaky, however, he was now travelling so fast that he was unable to negotiate the turn to the right at the bottom of the slope and he crashed into the railings. Sadly the tricycle did not survive the impact. The front wheel rolled off and the handle bars became twisted up in the railings. Beaky sobbed all the way home. He carried one half of his bike and I carried the other half, only I wasn't sobbing, I wasn't laughing; I might have had a bit of smirk on my face but I was definitely not laughing. In my opinion I thought the tricycle was a bit babyish, for lads of our calibre, and that he needed to man-up a bit more.

This loss, however, hit Beaky badly and his sobbing kept me awake for some time that night. I realised, then, that there was more to his hysteria than the loss of his tricycle. He accused me of deliberately sabotaging his bike because I didn't have one of my own and then he went back into sobbing mode again. After more tears he said that because I didn't bring anything with me from New Lodge I thought that I had a right to have his things, just like we had his tortoise Peter. I didn't want to get dragged into the tortoise saga with Beaky and I was getting a little fed up with him by now and so I rolled over in my bed. I suppose he must have eventually cried himself to sleep.

A new Dad, a pending visit and two bombshells are dropped

We had been living with our Mother for about two months when, one morning over breakfast, she announced that she had something important to ask us. Uncle Bill had already left for work as he was a self-employed builder and decorator. As we all assembled in the confined space of the kitchen our mother prepared breakfast. I remember thinking that this was the first time that she had done this since we had arrived. As we were all tucking in she told us that she had a couple of issues that needed to be dealt with.

The first concerned our relationship with Uncle Bill. At that point she began to open up to us about her association with him and that he had made huge sacrifices to have us living in this house. She went on to say that it would make life a lot easier for us all if we would now refer to him as Dad rather than Uncle Bill.

John commented "That we already have a Dad, Tenby, so why have another, and anyway where is Tenby and why doesn't he accept his share of the responsibility for us?"

She muttered something about him being a waste of space and that one of us should go with her to get her maintenance arrears from him.

She then added, "As you would all be enrolling into our new schools soon it would be so much easier and, simplify matters, if Uncle Bill was registered as our Dad."

I had no strong feelings one way or another and to suddenly switch and call him Dad rather than Uncle Bill seemed no real problem to me. I considered that we had already undergone a lot of emotional trauma and by comparison this was not a major issue.

She then asked George and John how they thought things were going and whether they had any issues that needed to be been raised by any of us. She did say how pleased she was that Beaky had been assimilated into our cohesive group and that we were looking out for him.

Speaking, on behalf of us all, George did say that the general consensus was that things were very different at Boston Road and that it would take time to get used to the differences as George was now twelve and John was fourteen. He said that the house was very cramped and the only place that we could all meet as a group was in the kitchen. In particular we all missed the day to day routine of our lives that we enjoyed when we were at New Lodge. Now that this had gone that we were finding it hard to deal with our new found freedom.

John said "That there were concerns over the free-for-all at breakfast" and dinner and that we all missed the regularity of our former mealtimes.

Finally I asked "that as some of us were still wearing our official 'outdoor' issue clothing, if we were to go to new schools would we need a uniform?"

Francis and I both thought that George's analysis of our new lives was pretty well spot on! Our mother, unfortunately, didn't quite accept our observations in the same way. She viewed them more like criticisms of her and Uncle Bill and rebuked us. She told us "that we were institutionalised and needed to get used to the idea of being freed from care. That she and Uncle Bill were doing their best under the circumstances and that as she worked we should try to help her out more."

It was at that moment that she dropped the first of two bombshells.

Apparently the 'follow-up' team, from Barnardo's, would be calling upon us and that we would each be spoken to, individually, by a social worker. She asked us to remember to express our gratitude for all they were trying to do for us and to tell the man or woman of any concerns that we might have or that continue to worry us. She then left for work.

On the day of the visit you would have thought that her Majesty herself was calling. We were woken up extra early by our mother, who decided that we needed clean bedding and that all the sheets were to be taken to the local launderette. She then insisted that we put our 'outdoor' clothes on and that we wore clean shirts and socks and then we waited together in the kitchen for the visitor to arrive. This was a familiar feeling for us and the anticipation tinged with the excitement made us all go into overdrive. Suddenly the doorbell rang. I thought it really odd because our mother suddenly started to speak as though she had a plum in her mouth as she invited the gentleman into the kitchen and offered him cup of tea.

I cannot remember anything of the conversation that I had with the social worker and that I was very happy with my situation, which seemed to be improving on a daily basis. Also I felt that as my relationship with Beaky had intensified I had become less reliant upon my older brothers and, for me, this was a good thing. Perhaps as we were growing up we were now, also, growing apart. I did feel as though I had developed a greater resistance to the issues that seemed to be concerning John and George so much. Especially doubts about our new lives in Walthamstow.

After the meeting we all had a family debriefing in the kitchen.

I remember that we were all there, including our new Dad and at no time was anything untoward ever mentioned. In fact our mother was very pleased as she thought that the visit had gone really well and that she was looking forward to the follow up visit to see if any recommendations had been made. Shortly afterwards the social worker contacted our Mother again to say that he had compiled his report, had a meeting with the after-care team at headquarters and wanted to come around again to discuss the recommendations that they would like to make. I sensed her concerns about the tone of the letter. She spoke to us all again and questioned us about any specifics that one or other of us may have raised. Again, George and John said nothing.

At this second meeting the social worker told us that he was very pleased with the way that the initial meeting had been conducted. He made a particular point of thanking our mother for her efforts in making us feel like members of her family.

The team were especially pleased with the way that Francis and I had settled in and that we were forming a stable relationship with our half-brother Martin and that we had no reservations in viewing Mr Beavis as our father. It was at that point that he suddenly dropped the second bombshell.

He explained that for the two oldest boys the situation was not quite the same. In fact George had such severe reservations about life in Boston Road that he had voluntarily asked to go back into the care of Barnardo's. Under the circumstances the team had no alternative but to listen to George, and his needs. It had been agreed, by all concerned, that he was to enrol at the Parkstone Sea Training School (a Barnardo run school) near to Parkstone in Poole and that he would need to be ready to begin his initial training when schools resumed again in one week's time. Our mother was shocked, not only by the fact that George had failed to tell her of his feelings but that he had discussed his situation with the team without any prior consultation with her.

The social worker informed us all that the Parkstone Sea Training School was formerly known as Russell Cotes Nautical School. That it had a good achievement record and that most boys left with good qualifications and the prospect of a career at Sea at the end of the training.

However, for our mother, there was more bad news to come!

Apparently John was also finding it increasingly difficult to adjust to life out of Barnardo's care. In particular he was finding the lack of routine at mealtimes and his general welfare very difficult to deal with. In short he was not able to cope with life on the "outside". One of his particular concerns was that when school resumed he would only have three months in the final year before leaving, as by then he would be 15 years old. He reckoned that over the years his education had suffered as a result of all the changes in his life. He was, after all, already attending school in Walthamstow when they were admitted into Barnardo's eight years earlier. He had concerns that the disruption that he faced now would impact upon him in adulthood especially when it came to securing a future career.

The Barnardo's visitor went on to tell our mother that he had discussed the options, with John, and that Barnardo's could offer him a similar option to the one that George had accepted. These ideas were dismissed by John but he did accept their offer of approved lodgings, and further one on one counselling, once he had reached the age of fifteen years of age.

So that was the outcome of his visit. George was now away at the Sea Training School in Dorset and John would shift between Boston Road and his new lodgings while attempting to keep a job down. It was decided that it would be best if John could return home as and when the need arose.

Once George had completed his initial pre-sea training he was allowed visitors and so one weekend we all went to Parkstone to see him. You can see in the picture, below, that Francis (in the middle) and I (left) were still dressing in our Barnardo's 'outsider' clothing. Actually we were becoming very conscious at having to wear short trousers as none of the boys around our area did and so we stood out a bit from the crowd. Beaky was wearing the dark jacket and Slugs is shown looking over our shoulders in his smart naval uniform. We were all pleased to meet up again and George seemed very settled in his new life.

Over the coming months Blamp and I underwent a slow process of enculturation. Beaky was already part of the local scene but things were different for us. We had to slowly learn and acquire the values and subtleties of life in Boston Road, our new schools and our new local environment. However, we adapted to our new surroundings and culture with some ease, undoubtedly helped by Beaky and his status within the local community of shops and residents.

It was Beaky who introduced me to one of the stalwarts of Boston Road, Old Ma Shep. Unfortunately for her she had no electricity supply in her house: it was run on gas alone. Her wireless ran on an accumulator battery and it was the recharging of her battery that was Beaky's, and then eventually my, responsibility to carry out. It involved us carrying it to the hardware shop, at the top of the road, where it was recharged overnight, to be collected the next day and reinstalled back into her wireless. She would give us sixpence for doing that for her.

Things were on the up for us. Once John moved into his digs things became a little more comfortable for the rest of us. Blamp was now able to move into John's bedroom and Beaky and I shared a bedroom.

One weekend evening, when both George and John were back at home, our mother and dad decided to go the pictures and gave John two bob to look after us. He decided that it would be fun if we all sat around the wireless to listen to a new series called 'Journey into Space'. He said that he had been listening to it in his lodgings and that it was enthralling. It was set in 1965, the year when it was reckoned that man would first walk on the Moon, and that we could hear all of the episodes by listening to the BBC Light Programme. He went on to tell us that once the rocket had actually set off for the Moon the programme began to attract an enormous number of listeners. He then gave us a brief summary of what we were going to hear. He dimmed the lights a little and pulled the curtains over, just to create the right atmosphere, and then he said:

"It is 1965, and Jet's father launches his A.24 rocket from the Rocket Research Station (R.R.S). However things go wrong and the rocket suddenly starts to head out of control towards Las Vegas. It hits the town, killing many people, and as a result the RRS is closed down. Meanwhile, Jet is invited by Mitch to join his Operation Luna project – a rocket to reach the Moon."

Well, after about ten minutes of sitting absolutely still Beaky and I became restless and a bit fidgety and started to make monster noises which annoyed John. We were only having a giggle to relieve the boredom. I said that I wanted to listen to something else, upon which John took a real swipe at the two of us. I was shocked because I thought that it was quite a spiteful attack upon us. Anyway we decided that we would do something on our own in the kitchen and left George, Francis and John to their boring wireless.

The next day we went for a walk and George joined us, just before his return from leave from the Training School, and as usual our mother had her trusty box camera at hand to record the moment (below). In this photograph you can clearly see that our former official Barnardo 'uniform' had been replaced with jeans, a snake-belt (all the rage then) and casual jumpers. I have my arms around a friend, Alan (on my right) and Beaky (on my left), with Blamp on the extreme right and George behind us all. You can also observe how George had grown so much over the passing weeks of his training.

I do remember thinking that he had undergone a change and seemed less carefree than he was. It was as if he had the world on his shoulders in spite of being in his preferred environment. I also thought that although I missed him a lot these feelings were not reciprocated. Still with a new school to join there was still much to do!

Public baths, a new School and fisticuffs!

Another down side of London living was that we had no bathroom at Boston Road so unless we had been swimming we had to use the public baths on a fairly regular basis. Like most teenage lads Beaky and I were both fairly fastidious youths and so we would wash ourselves in the kitchen sink on a fairly regular basis, at least once a week, whether it was needed or not!. That was, unless, we had been swimming and we could take shower there.

Anyway we would alternate our usual "cleansing routine" with a trip to the Leyton Public Baths near to the Baker Arms (below). You paid your money and were usually given a towel and a small bar of soap. You then gave your ticket to the bath-man who would direct you to a cubicle that contained, hopefully, a bath full of clean hot water.

As I was about to enrol at my new school, with Beaky, our mother sent us off to have a good soak and clean up. As we entered the baths we usually liked to check out our neighbours so that we could have some fun at the same time. As the bath water began to cool down one could ask the bath-man for extra hot water at no cost and he would use a universal attachment that fitted to the outside wall of the cubicle to control the water. On this particular occasion we were both up for some merry-making. Beaky noticed that he had a gentleman in the next cubicle to him and so he shouted out "More hot water in number four please". After about five minutes he made the same request until we heard the poor gentleman shouting out "no more hot water please in number four".

I then turned my attentions to the gentleman in number six and played the same trick upon him. Of course we both felt that this was the funniest thing that we had done since the last time we had done something as stupid and irresponsible.

As we left the baths the bath-man approached us and asked "if we were the little buggers who were asking for extra hot water".

"Nah not us guv" replied Beaky and then as we both made a bee-line for the exit Beaky called back to him "Oh guv-more hot in number four please".

Our mother kept on and on to us both about the need to be at the school (next page), in Gamuel Road, in good time so that I could get my school photograph taken. She had to go with Francis to the junior school.

We both turned up in good time and found our respective classes. Some of the lads began questioning me as to why I was only just turning up for class and where I had been during the previous year. I decided that fantasy was the best response and so instead of going on about

Barnardo's and the homes I kept it simple. "My dad's a train driver and so we have to move around the country with his job". That was all it took to stop the questions and now all I needed was to ensure that Beaky corroborated my story.

Being a new face in the classroom I became conscious of lots of stares from the other children but my greatest reservation came from the fact that the class was mixed. What's more I had a girl sitting right next to me. I was struck by her tiny hands and that her skin looked very soft. This was a new experience for me and I liked it, I liked it a lot. I thought she was very pretty with long fair hair and her name was Gloria.

I don't know why but at that moment I began to wonder about Anthony, my friend from the Bray Wood School, and then about Beaky and what he was doing. Suddenly, my day dreaming came to abrupt end when I heard my name being mentioned. I looked around the classroom and realised that the teacher was looking at me.

"Well William, are you going to tell us or not?" she said. I had no idea what she was talking about but decided to bluff it.

"Of course I will," I replied.

"Well, get on with it laddy".

"Get on with what?" I replied.

"Telling us where you come from and what has bought you to our school today" she said.

I looked at Gloria, who was looking at me, and I blushed. This was definitely a new experience. I coughed out aloud, cleared my throat and decided to "wing-it" when I told them that "As Beaky was in the class below me our mother decided it is best for me to be here with him so that I can keep my eye on him and keep him from getting into any further trouble".

She seemed to be quite satisfied with my response and she never raised an eyebrow about who he was or what trouble, if any, he had caused. I thought that in general I was pretty good at bluffing my way out of problems. After this episode we all went to see the school photographer and I saw Beaky there with his school chums.

He seemed to be popular and very well assimilated within his group of friends, whereas I was at a bit of a loose end especially when it came to talking with girls. Oh, how I was missing my old school!

I spoke to Beaky about Gloria and that I liked her, although we hadn't yet spoken to each other, and that she had very pretty hair. Beaky reckoned that I was at least two years behind him, when it came to girls, and that he had already been to Saturday Matinee with Gloria and that he liked her as well, along with lots of other girls. I was a bit taken back by his bluntness. We each had our photographs taken and when they came back I was pleasantly surprised and thought that they had come out great, especially the one of Beaky (on the left).

Later that morning I met up with him again as we queued for our lunches. I am not too sure of the reason why but both of us were entitled to free school dinners. The problem for me was that we had to declare this every day in the class room as our teachers had the responsibility for collecting the monies and needed to know who was entitled to a freebie. I always thought that there was a stigma attached to having to make such a public declaration like that in front of your fellow pupils. In the playground those that had a free dinner entitlement were thought of as the lowest of low, and I didn't like to be thought of in that way. I had put up with that already when I was a Barnardo boy!

Anyway, we were patiently waiting in the queue for lunch, one of the boys in my class decided that he didn't want to queue with us. With his friends he marched right up to the front of the queue. When I mentioned this to Beaky he surprised me by telling me just to stand back and just let it go. In all of my experience in the homes there was only one way of dealing with bullies who thought that they could get away with whatever they wanted and that was to confront them. I walked up to the front of the queue and politely asked him what he thought he was doing. He looked at me and uttered some bad words and told me to mind my own business as this was what he always did and nobody had stopped him before. I, again, politely told him that it would be in his very best interests to simply wander back to his rightful pace in the queue and that we would forget that this had ever happened. He asked me whether I wanted to pick up my teeth off of the ground with broken fingers.

Now despite my tender years I still considered that as rather a serious threat, so I suggested to him that the next meal he took might be through a straw on a hospital ward and then the punch up started.

126

'Bundle'! I heard coming from behind me and all of the children stood around us egging us on. I guess that secretly, deep down, we all liked a bundle provided you were watching it and were not a participant. Then one becomes full of bravado and as I looked around at our 'admirers' Beaky was there shouting out on the top of his voice "Go on Tubs give him a good pasting".

Our fight didn't last too long but the dinner ladies ran away in horror. I was actually on top of the little reprobate letting him taste the back of my knuckles when I suddenly felt myself being wrenched off of him bodily by a teacher. I can't even remember what the outcome was but it couldn't have been that serious because we both had lunch, and what's more he never jumped the queue again. In fact, although he decided that I was better ally than a foe, he never looked me straight in the eyes ever again.

I reckon that this was justice – Walthamstow style!

Blimey Tubs and Beaky have "morphed" into one!

I have thought about that bundle many times and to me it marks a significant turning point in my young adolescent life. The linchpin on that day was Beaky, not John, not George and not Francis - it was my younger brother Beaky and it was Beaky who was the bridge in my life between Barnardo's, which was slowly becoming dimmer but not disappearing from view, and my new life in Walthamstow.

For the first time I felt that I was in a place where I belonged, where I could be who I wanted to be and with the freedom to grow and extend my wings in the way that I wanted. Over the coming years Beaky and I spent many a happy time up the forest (Epping) or down the river (Lea), and during that time together we kind of morphed into each other as you can probably tell from this photograph.

Gone were the itchy little suits, the brylcreemed hair and the dominance of my older brothers. Now I felt pleased to wear jeans and a sloppy joe or a lumberjack shirt, all the rage then, and wearing bumpers from Woolworths on my feet. I am the one on the right. I now considered myself to be a Walthamstow lad with my own identity, and do you know what? I loved it. We had some good times together growing up in Boston Road, and although it was not always a bed of roses it was our bed to lie in and we made the best of it. My memories of Barnardo's have gradually faded and become dimmer with age but they have never faded from view entirely.

So what about old *Tyke* - well he was a figment of my imagination.
Teddy - I miss him every day and still wonder what happened to him.
Nurse Nasty - I have a lot of respect for carbolic soap but will not let it near to my mouth!
Ashley Coombe - just a patch of scrubland on a Somerset hillside.
Anthony - well I wrote a couple of times but never got a reply. I guess that, like me, he settled into his new life.
Ronuk - who were those Large Eggs kidding! It took weeks to get rid of it and what's more it didn't work! C'est la vie!

I have to say that Windsor Way now seems a
LONG
LONG
LONG
LONG way away

Over and out for now!

Mum with John, her first born, 1940

CHAPTER SIX

Post-Script – Rationale

In this finale to my tome I want to explore three issues.

The first, concerns the impact that our time in the care of Barnardo's had upon me. Where possible I will attempt to explore its effect upon my older brothers as well.

The second, concerns the effect of our presence, along with the 'Barnardo effect' upon our move into Boston Road, in particular, how we affected the dynamics of the new family.

The third will be a brief description of our post-Barnardo lives and what effectively, became of us all.

"You can take the boy out of Barnardo's but you cannot take Barnardo's out of the boy"

I am sure that you are familiar with the idea being expressed in this quotation for instance, with reference, to the military however complementary to this expression are other equally meaningful quotations like this one from 'The Philosophy of Aristotle' who said, "Give me a child until he is seven and I will show you the Man". Likewise with the Jesuits. Another one suggests that 'Once you are a Barnardo Boy you are Barnardo's for life'.

So what truth, if any, are there in these expressions?

Being a Barnardo "graduate" it was relatively easy to identify those indicators of the Barnardo legacy. Perhaps a few of the most important legacies remain to this day for instance fair play, honesty and integrity and above all respect for elders. Less obvious were just how formal we tended to be in all ways for instance in the way we addressed our elders. Thus my acquaintances in the horological world were always Mr Bide and Mr Bugden (Buggie) rather than Charlie or Roland respectively. Once we were out of our teen's denim Jeans were relegated and replaced by smart trousers/corduroys, Tweed jackets with leather patch elbows and a shirt and tie, no casualness here!! Also none of us were really interested in team sports, or any sports come to that, and the youth culture of the times such as the music scene and discos past us by completely. Reminiscing about our life and times in Barnardo's still remains high on the agenda of topics to discuss when we all get together again.

During my writings I became very interested in exploring two interrelated facts about our former time in care, particularly in relation to the above quotations.

The first was to gain an understanding of how our experience of living in Barnardo's care may have impacted upon us all as individuals. I was the only one, out of the four of us, who was a baby and was therefore less exposed to the "toxic" environment in Woodend Road. Was it possible, therefore, that life in the care of Barnardo's would impact less upon me than it did upon my siblings? I was, after all, a fairly blank sheet in terms of development. My older siblings would still have retained a distant memory of life with our parents prior to 1946, and I became convinced that through our unique experience as four young siblings in Barnardo's care I should be in a strong position to explore this a little further.

Secondly I wanted to explore just how our experience of life in care impacted upon the lives of those with whom we lived with and associated with after we left New Lodge. We all recognised that there would have to have been a great deal of understanding and give and take on all sides within the new family unit.

I was never convinced that we had much give and take in fact we were probably quite unyielding after all in the homes we had all of our thinking done for us and we had never had to reach a decision on our own. It seemed that our mother and Bill would have to be flexible and undertake most of the yielding. It follows from this that any form of repatriation that was based on anything other than love, yearning, wanting and needing would almost certainly fail. In contrast to this scenario if it were based upon guilt, previous poor judgements or simply through naïve expectations, a breakdown in relationships would be inevitable.

So, looking back in time I think that there were a few tell-tale signs coming to the fore that relate to this scenario and identified in Chapter 5. It was at that stage, when we had only been back in the family home for a few months, that our older two siblings expressed the difficulties that they were experiencing in settling down in the outside world after eight years of institutionalised care. In the case of one, he was anxious to return back to Barnardo's care almost immediately; the second sought an entirely different experience.

It would appear that although they had been taken out of the care of Barnardo's, and then repatriated into the family environment, this alone was not sufficient for them. Their time in the homes had made a deep and lasting impression but, in spite of the support of their younger siblings, it was not enough. The intensely strong pull of their former life in care and the positive influence it had upon them was clearly overwhelming. It was their comfort blanket and they were not yet ready or prepared to give it up. This is what I refer to when I talk about the "Barnardo effect". As it happened, the two of them had also experienced a family life before Barnardo's and so that may also have played a significant role.

The key issue here, however, seems to be an inability to adapt to the sudden changes in their lives as rapidly as Francis and I were able. It is as if there was a mismatch between their expectations of what a family life at Boston Road should have been like and the reality of their Barnardo family. The former was unable to fulfil the aims and objectives of the latter.

In contrast I didn't experience the same sense of disappointment with my new situation. It is true that I had some misgivings in the very early stages and I very much missed the spaciousness of New Lodge and my school friends, especially Anthony. However I also felt that Francis and I were very, very, lucky because we were closer in age to Martin than we were to John and George, and with that came adaptability. I am convinced that it was Martin's support and guidance, during the very early days at Boston Road, which instilled a level of confidence in us both.

In fact we all needed each other.

Beaky needed us, so that he could show us off to his chums and let them know that he had big brothers to care for him and to fight his corner. As far as Francis and I were concerned we had an ally who could show us the ropes. As a result of our new found confidence and independence we were able to do something that John and George were unable to do. In contrast to their situation we were both able to loosen the hold that the homes previously had on us whilst grabbing ever tightly to the new ones in Walthamstow.

I would not like you to think, for one moment, that George and John were ever deliberately excluded from our circle or that we ring-fenced ourselves to the exclusion of them both. That would be an untruth. In reality they allowed the situations to pass them by through inertia. In New Lodge they were the big cheeses and now they were not. One way for them to get along, and face their new situation, would have been with the help of their youngest half-brother. It seems that their preference was to seek a new life elsewhere.

In the meantime Francis and I went out everywhere with Beaky and, unknowingly, we were gradually became socially culturalised within our new environment. As a consequence of this change in attitude to our new found life, the earlier period in Barnardo's, which John and George seemed to be clinging on to, was eventually knocked off of the top spot for us and replaced by our new life in Boston Road. Personally, I think that is what the Barnardo family team would have wanted a gradual weaning from their apron strings.

In fact the only time that I believe we were ever ring-fenced, as a group, was actually when we were in care. It was as if an invisible thread interconnected between us and that together we would move through places, not as individuals, but as a quartet, headed by John. Certainly when I went out on my own without them, like my first day at school, I felt anxious and had real concerns and fears. Once we had arrived at Boston Road, however, we had Beaky, our 'reality check', who served as a conduit, a bridge to link us between our former life in care and our new life in Walthamstow.

He was the local lad who knew the area like the back of his hand, and yet our relationship as brothers had been allowed to flourish. Without meaning to embarrass him, when he actually reads this, it was only through writing this narrative that I was able to rationalise my feelings and emotions during this period of transition. It was Beaky who put me in my place, who brought me back down to earth and made me get off of my 'high horse'. He reminded me that just because I spoke differently and had ideals above my station in life I was not, in fact, an aristocrat or a member of the landed gentry but an oik like him!

He went on to remind me that I was just a young lad, an urchin like him, making my way through a new way of life!

It was also Beaky who showed me the ropes, how to navigate the stormy seas of conflict, to walk the walk, to talk the talk and, with help from my Barnardo's background, to run with the fox and hunt with the pack. We lads may not always have shown how we felt about Beaky to his face and I was sincerely sorry about his tricycle and about Peter the tortoise; but it was an expression of my newfound brotherly love that saved him from a jolly good smacking when he wouldn't stop snivelling about the trike and keeping me awake!

To me that was true brotherly love Barnardo/Walthamstow style.

It was inevitable that we would be unable to spend such a significant part of our childhood in the care of the Barnardo's homes without the situation bearing a major influence upon us. At family gatherings it rapidly becomes the topic of conversations as we reminisce, with great fondness, the anecdotes that I have shared with you. In my particular case my background taught me a lot about fair play and even-handedness. For me the need for punctuality, always to do my best and to try as hard as I could to succeed, coupled with basic honesty and integrity, were paramount. I consider these to be valuable legacies from my time in Barnardo's and these, I reckon, to be the positive side of the "Barnardo effect".

Gwendoline Beatrice Farrow-Tyrrell. Our mother

Our mother was born in 1918 into an upper working class family in Walthamstow in Essex. She was undoubtedly a very attractive young lady and by the time she was 28 she had four sons with our father Tenby. It was never really made clear to us, or perhaps we just never really asked the right sort of questions at the time, why nobody in our extended family ever intervened to prevent us going into care in the first place. We have often thought that her need to get married was a key factor. At the time there was a very different attitude towards pre-marital relationships and her family may have adopted a hard-hearted approach that 'She had made her bed so now she must lie in it; However, that outlook never really explained why none of her siblings or our grand-parents ever made any form of contact throughout the eight years that we were in Barnardo's, which will always remain a mystery to us.

The first impression that I had of our mother was one that was formed months earlier when she came to visit us in New Lodge. Then, as ever, she was unreliable and unpunctual. When we were told that she was scheduled to pay us a visit she was inevitably late or, as on several occasions, would fail to turn up at all.

Deep down I remember questioning her motives for our return. I can honestly say that she never found it easy having us all back there and we certainly didn't make it easy for her with our constant questioning and comparisons with our former life in care. We not only placed a great financial and emotional burden upon the household but we had a dramatic effect upon the existing family dynamics.

Beaky was the only child who was used to a fairly close and intimate relationship with his parents. Then we turn up on the scene and he went from being the only child to being one of five, and the youngest at that, the lowest in the new pecking order. As if that wasn't enough we all came with our own 'baggage', into the family unit, and with each of us having 'chips on our shoulders', that would fill Epping Forest. These must have added a further level of complexity to the household.

It was inevitable, therefore, that at some time or another the stresses between us all would become intolerable. This was a pressure cooker waiting to blow.

One of the first impositions that resulted from our homecoming was that my mother and Bill Beavis lost their own bedroom. Boston Road was too small to accommodate us all and so they had to sleep in the sitting room. Consequently the only place where we could congregate together was the kitchen-scullery.

Our mother would certainly agree with me when I say that she was not really cut out for motherhood as such. From the dialogue between her and Tenby that she seemed happy to share with us, her first four sons were a consequence rather than a planned-for event. Paradoxically she was a woman that seemed to be haunted and guilt-ridden by her past actions and yet unprepared to learn from them.

Tensions within the household were inevitable and mealtimes could be stressful as she was not too well domesticated. If it couldn't be fried we wouldn't have it. It seemed to me that the preparation for a typical Sunday lunch of bangers and mash with gravy would begin at about 11.30 am. This would be accompanied, with copious amounts of complaining, that she was just a skivvy around the house. Usually around 3.00 pm, just when we had given up any notion of being fed, she would call out to us that our dinner was ready. One of her favourite "pièces de résistance" would then occur if we failed to respond. Sometimes she would say nothing more, but more usually she would repeat this again, and if we were still not at the table, pronto, we would hear smash, smash, smash and all the plates of bangers and mash would be sliding down the rear garden wall.

On other occasions she would decide that she needed to 'change the beds' at 11.00 pm, when we were all in bed, or hoover the place from top to bottom in the middle of the night. Unfortunately, there were times when family niggles and other constraints became too much and there would be a blazing row. She would accuse us of being ungrateful little buggers and then threaten to send us back to Barnardo's. Which upset us greatly.

In fact we began to feel a certain resentment that she would hold such a threat over us. Having said that, I fully accept that we were a handful in her home however, we were her handful and nobody else's. Although we were only children we were her children and her responsibility! We have already seen that her two eldest sons were not able to acclimatise to their new life in Walthamstow. However it is my understanding that this was more as a result of their inability to settle down rather than any fault of our mother.

The problem with raising children is that in most cases people must learn how to do it through practice. When one suddenly finds the nest of three, filled with four others, to make a nest of seven, the task of parenthood becomes an even greater challenge. If, for a whole number of reasons, the person is inadequate or simply incapable of coping, then the challenge can develop into a battle, and, not necessarily between mother and siblings. Over time, our mother's loyalties began to cause fractures in her relationships with others in her family.

On a more positive note we did enjoy regular trips to Canvey Island or Southend even though her tardiness always meant that we were late in getting away. Typically we would be told to get ready for a trip to the seaside in good time. However; inevitably we would then be kept waiting for hours, for her to get ready. Then, as we were about to leave, she would suddenly remember that she had left a window open or that the back door was left open, meaning that we had to return. Eventually we would arrive at our destination in the late afternoon.

There was, however, a positive legacy from our mother and that was an interest in music and the piano. We had an upright piano in the sitting room which our mother could play like a good'un. Her favourite artiste was Winifred Atwell and she would play her music as we sat looking on and listening in awe. Inevitably, as we shall see, music became a significant focus in our lives as well.

The picture (below) was one of the last to be taken of our mother with four of her sons. It was taken in 1993 when Penny, her eldest granddaughter and the daughter of Martin, was married.

Left to right: John, William (Tubs), our mother (front), Francis (Blamp) and Martin (Beaky) right.

Sadly our mother died in 1998 but many of her foibles and skills live on in her 9 grandchildren, 9 great grandchildren and 2 great, great grandchildren.

Cyril William Beavis – Uncle and Stepfather

Unfortunately we knew very little about Uncle Bill except that he came from a Norfolk farming family. He was born in 1910 and died in 1965 at the age of 54. From my earliest recollections his interactions with us was on a limited basis. Having said that, parent–child relationships were on a different footing back in the fifties. Today the new 'good-bye' seems to be 'love you'; well that's what they all seem to say on the TV. Anyway, back then, men held their feelings much closer to their chests. Bill was a self-employed builder and decorator and so was out of the house for most of the day. However I do remember him telling us that he was happy to put a roof over our heads but that the rest was up to Tenby, a very generous gesture on his part.

I have always thought that once we were on the scene Bill was between a rock and hard place with our mother and the relationships that she was attempting to create her four other sons. I believe that the best scenario for Uncle Bill would have been just him and our Mother to be living, as a family of three with Martin, in their terraced Walthamstow home. Life would have been much more affordable and the house would have still offered the three of them all the space they needed. Although I would love to have believed that he was a generous philanthropist, with his heart focused upon our repatriation together, this suggestion doesn't really hold water. So what were his motivations for taking us on-board?

My understanding was that our mother was his life and that his devotion towards her knew no bounds. So once they had acquired everything that they thought was needed for us to return to the fold they went for it. The wanting and yearning, however, were all from our mother. Bill was giving our mother what she thought she really wanted and that was us back in her life. I suppose that, in reality, we came as part of the package deal!

We had many pictures of them together but, to me, this is the very essence of Bill as I knew and remembered him. It was taken by Francis in the mid-fifties at Wanstead Flats. It shows a devoted couple but is everything what it seems? In the picture our mother reveals a slight smile however "Bill" seldom smiled. He always looked very serious. I always thought that his sad, almost melancholy, demeanour was a result of dissatisfaction at some time in his life. It was as though he was carrying a 'heavy load'. Having said that, it would be easy to blame us and suggest that his burden was our mothers four other sons, but I am not convinced.

We were living with them because our mother wanted it that way; probably Barnardo's were quite keen too. "Bill" was prepared to do anything to secure her happiness and so we were accepted by him. That is not to say that there were not issues and threats but these were, perhaps, inevitable under the circumstances.

Perhaps of more relevance were some discoveries that we made about his past life. We learned that Bill had an extremely punishing experience as a Prisoner of War during the Second World War. We are all, now, convinced that the hazardous working conditions, he met during his imprisonment in a slave labour camp, contributed to his untimely death at the age of 54. Today Post-Traumatic-Stress Disorder (PTSD) has received worldwide recognition as a condition in its own right. However; back in the 1940s and the 1950s it was not officially acknowledged.

When he was eventually demobbed, from the Army, he was informed that, like thousands of other servicemen before him, he was not to talk about his wartime experiences. Effectively he was told to get on with life on his own. No form of counselling was offered to him and he was left to negotiate life with his 'battle scars' completely on his own. It is no wonder that his general 'joie de vivre', during the latter part of his life, became affected.

There were some brighter moments in his life, however, they seemed to be focused upon having some fun at our expense. I was never really sure whether this was his way of having a laugh or whether he was genuinely seeking revenge upon us!

I remember one particular incident, in the early 1950s, when the Moscow State Circus came to the Haringey Arena. This was a big event as it was the first time that a state circus from the Soviet Union had visited Western Europe and we had tickets to go. During the intermission Beaky and I asked Bill if we could get some ice creams. Initially he said no. However, as the queue began to get longer and longer, he suddenly pulled out some coinage and told us to get some choc ices. However by that time the queue was so long that we had to wait nearly twenty minutes for our turn. We gave the usherette our money and she said, "Sorry Sonny, we don't take Irish pennies".

We looked up at "Bill" and he was falling about laughing at us.

In hindsight we have all had a lot of time to reflect about our relationship with Bill. Francis reckoned that we could have treated him more kindly and that we took him for granted. I certainly felt that I was argumentative, even confrontational with him, and this I regret. In hindsight I feel that he made an honourable and noble decision, out of love for our mother, but failed to appreciate fully the repercussions of all that he was taking on. It is therefore all credit to him that he chose to make the sacrifices, on our behalf; and for that I will always be grateful. I do wish that I could tell him of my feelings for him today.

Martin Cyril Beavis – Our Half-brother

Martin always held the consistent view that he couldn't wait for us to join the happy household in Walthamstow; that we would be his friends and companions and keep him from harm, and everything would be rosy in the garden.

In reality he reckoned that our return brought him disappointment, and emotional upset and that we were not the pillars of support that we were supposed to be. He told me that before we left Barnardo's care he felt like an only child and afterwards, once we were living with him in Walthamstow, he still felt the same and that he didn't feel part of our group. It's that 'Barnardo effect' again.

What was interesting to me was that his interpretation of events was in sharp contrast to my own. I was always of the opinion that we did much together and enjoyed each other's company.

Perhaps Beaky also needed time to acclimatise to us as well!

He has also spoken of the vivid memories that he harboured of the haranguing that we gave him on many topics. That we always thought that we were right and that he was wrong and that we would coerce and brow-beat him into change. He also reminded me of the various ways that the way would try to scare him.

Our favourite tactic involved Francis and I disappearing and hiding in our bedroom shortly before Beaky was due to go to bed. Being the youngest he would have to go up before any of us and so we would pre-empt this. Usually I would hide under the bed and Francis in the wardrobe. We knew when Beaky was coming because the hall light would go on and he would call out good-night to his parents as he went upstairs. As he came into the room I would grab his ankles, which usually had the desired effect of making him scream at the top of his voice.

Then as he went to the wardrobe to get his jim-jams Francis would be hiding in there to give him a 'double dose of fear'.

I remember another occasion, just when he thought that he had "sussed" our little game, when I pretended to everybody, except Francis, that I was out for the whole evening. I decided that I would give Beaky a real surprise and while he thought I was out I was actually lying in wait under his bed ready to ambush him. When he eventually came up to bed I was there waiting, and true to form, Beaky didn't disappoint and had to rush to the bathroom screaming. In hindsight I can now see what he meant about feeling emotionally horrible and, I have to say, that he had full justification for thinking like that.

Like most working class children we were both minor members of the ABC and would attend Saturday morning pictures at the local cinema every Saturday morning while wearing our badge with pride.

'The ABC Minors' was a Saturday cinema club for children in the 1950s. At the beginning of each session we would all sing the 'ABC Minors Song' (page i). The lyrics were shown on the screen with a little 'ball' that bounced along, above the words, in time with the music (Karaoke-style).

"We are the boys and girls well known as

Minors of the ABC

And every Saturday all line up

To see the films we like, and shout aloud with glee

We like to laugh and have a singsong

Such a happy crowd are we.

We're all pals together.

We're minors of the A-B-C"

(shout A-B-C extra loudly).

One particular Saturday morning sticks out vividly in my memory. We were both heading to the local cinema to enjoy the Saturday matinee and it was snowing quite heavily and we were both wearing our Wellington boots. Unfortunately, for Beaky, he dropped his sixpence into the snow and, despite all of our efforts, we were unable to retrieve it again. Beaky was desperately upset and began to snivel passionately making his balaclava look a right mess. He looked up at me in a state of despair and said words to the effect that our mother's never going to give him another tanner and so not only had he spoiled his chances of going to the cinema but that he had also stymied mine as well. Beaky had, unfortunately, made a rather false assumption, that just because he wasn't able go to the cinema I wouldn't either! With words of comfort and reassurance I said to him,

"Don't worry that you can't go Beaky; it's alright, I will just go by myself instead. See you back at home".

Yes, I guess he did have reason to resent us; especially me!

There were many good times though and on another Saturday morning Beaky entered a yoyo competition at the cinema. I never realised that he actually owned a yo-yo yet alone that he had winning 'moves'. Although he was reluctant to show me he did have a 'pièce de résistance' which, he reckoned, should help him to lift the prize. During the intermission he was called to go onto the cinema stage and perform all of his tricks in front of the young cinema goers. His speciality was called 'walking the dog'.

He had performed most of his tricks and was just psyching himself for the climax of his performance. I sensed his confidence and I am sure that Beaky thought that the competition was his and that it was in the bag. Anyway as he flicked his right hand out, to release the yo-yo from the palm of his hand, he gave it his magic tug that sent it cascading, in a spin down onto the stage. In the final phase the yo-yo should have rolled along the stage with the string looking like a 'dogs lead' (above), hence walking the dog. All the kids were looking on in astonishment as they hadn't seen anything like this before. However, to Beaky's horror, the string unwound completely and the yo-yo ran along the length of the stage with all of the string following on behind.

It continued to roll right to the end of the stage and then fell off. His moment of glory was over.

The promotor looked at Beaky and told him that he was disqualified. Kids being kids started to jeer him and then shouted for him to 'Get off of the stage'. Poor Beaky was in such a state and, true to form, started to snivel. I left my seat to meet him in the aisle and I gave him a cuddle of support.

As we were leaving the cinema the winner of the yo-yo competition was in the foyer showing the children some of his tricks. The publicity machine was there taking photographs of him when his friends started to heckle Beaky and called out to him that he was loser.

Alas all of my good work was wasted when he started to blub again. Actually I thought that their treatment of him was rather harsh, as although his finale let him down, most of his other tricks with the yo-yo were outstanding. Anyway I had enough of their 'attitude' to my little 'bruv' and thought that I should step up to the mark and let them all know that if they cheeked Beaky then they were cheeking me to.

I said to the heckler "He's my brother, don't you know! I think you need to tell him that his efforts were appreciated and that it was a pity that his string broke. It could have happened to anyone couldn't it?"

I gave the lad a dirty look and eyed his yo-yo up and down threateningly at that he ran off. Beaky had his justice.

One Saturday our mother gave us some extra pocket money, so not only could we afford to attend the Saturday matinee but we also had enough money left over to conclude our fantastic day with a delicious pie and mash lunch at Manse's pie and eel shop up at the Bakers Arms. Pie and mash was traditional working-class food with its origins in the East End of London. It was usual for the mashed potato to be spread around one side of the plate and for green liquor, traditionally made using the liquid retained from the preparation of the stewed eels, to be poured over the pie. For us this was a perfect end to our morning and an event to remain in the 'good memory' bank, as opposed to the other one. I reckon that, upon reflection, things were not that bad for us both after all. My greatest wish is that Beaky might now agree with me.

and the rest of us?

Front: Beaky (left), Blamp (right). Back: Tubs (left), Slugs, John (right)

This is probably the only picture that shows all five of us brothers together in one place. It was taken at Beaky's house, in Hemel Hempstead, in about 2005 and it is unlikely that such a reunion, with all five of us together, will ever take place again.

As a young man John had a variety of jobs but always seemed to find it hard to be punctual. Later on though he secured a job in social work before eventually training to become a piano tuner, a job that he continues to do today at the age of eighty. He lives in the Midlands with his wife, two children and two granddaughters. John also has a further son and daughter plus two grandchildren from a previous marriage. Music continues to play a significant part in his life and the life of his family. As well as John and his wife, Helen, enjoy concerts and recitals Helen also plays the piano and their daughter conducts the Redditch ladies' choir.

George (Slugs, centre-back) decided not to go to sea and instead he went to college before becoming the only Tyrrell boy to go to University. He lives a quiet life in Buckinghamshire with his two sons.

Francis (Blamp, front right) also has a great interest in music. After school he spent many years working in the Russian Book Shop in Museum Street, London. Eventually, in his mid-twenties, he studied piano restoration and tuning at the London College of Furniture before embarking upon a career as a tuner and restorer. Francis acquired an eclectic taste in classical music and has one of the largest collections of classical CDs and music memorabilia in the country. He has a particular fondness for early 20th century Russian composers and pianists as well as their British counterparts especially Benjamin Britten, John Ireland and Frank Bridge. A particularly favourite work is 'Opus clavicembalisticum' a 1930 work for solo piano composed by Kaikhosru Shapurji Sorabji. It is renowned for its length and difficulty and is the longest piano piece in existence, 4 - 4½ hours, depending on tempo. If you can acquire copy of this particular work I challenge you to sit all the way through it.

Francis retired from West London to the Kent coast in 2010.

Martin (Beaky, front left) followed in his father's' footsteps and spent his adult life in the building trade. Martin has a weakness for vintage and luxury cars and currently enjoys travelling around, visiting his family, in his Bentley with his wife. He has an extensive family, having become a father for the first time when he was only sixteen, and has three daughters, five grandchildren and two great grandchildren.

And now to me, William (Bill) (Tubs, rear left) I left George Gascoigne School, formerly Queens Road School, at the age of 15, in 1961. With the help, guidance and support of Mr James Dixon, the headmaster, I attained a School Leaving Certificate. At fifteen years of age I applied to join the regular Army, the Junior Leaders Regiment, but my historic ear trouble let me down and this resulted in a failed medical. On the rebound I applied to join the Merchant Navy, passed the medical and went to the National Sea Training School at Sharpness, in Gloucestershire, in June 1962 (below). The training ship was called the Vindicatrix. It was a former sailing ship and was moored in Sharpness from 1939 to 1966 to provide a base for training boys as deck hands and stewards for the merchant navy. The courses lasted two or three months, and around 70,000 boys, called Vindi boys, received their basic training there.

After I had completed my three months pre-sea training I then went to sea on my first voyage to Canada on board the SS Alsatia, of the Cunard line. My second, and longer voyage, was aboard the Port Line ship the Port Invercargill. This took me, initially, to the Dutch West Indies and then travelling, via the Panama Canal, across the Pacific Ocean to New Zealand. However, by the time that I was nineteen years of age I realised I needed to gain a foothold back home and to secure a future for myself and reached the decision that my time at sea should draw to an end.

Like my brothers I was also very dexterous and eventually went into the technical side of theatre work in London. I worked for many years at the Jeanette Cochrane Theatre in Holborn before returning to Higher Education, in Holborn, with the intention of becoming a teacher.

Distractions, such as marriage to Lizzie, thwarted my plans and I sought employment at St Thomas's Hospital in London, working for the Engineer's Department. It was while I was working there that I met the resident Horologist, yes St Thomas's employed their own clockmaker at that time, Mr Charles Bide, who took me under his wing and set me off on a new career as a Watch and Clockmaker. This year, 2020, I will celebrate nearly fifty years of running my own antique clock business, and for the past thirty years this has been in Midhurst in West Sussex.

During the intervening years I was able to fulfil some of the ambitions, which I had harboured as a child, but was thwarted from following for one reason or another. These include learning to fly, I gained my private Pilot's licence (PPL) in 1982.

In the same year I became an A class radio ham and Morse examiner for the Radio Society of Great Britain (RSGB). I also satisfied my ambition for the police force when I became a Special Constable in 1976. I served in the Wiltshire Police, while living on Salisbury Plain, before transferring to the Hampshire Police in 1977, when I moved my business to Lee on the Solent in Hampshire.

This photograph was taken for a publicity campaign to recruit more Special Constables for the Hampshire Constabulary.

In 1982 an opportunity arose for me to consider a change in my extracurricular interests when I took a short break away from the Specials in order to fulfil a lifelong dream to join the Army. This time it was in the Royal Military Police (TA) (below).

By 1984 it was back into the Police again, as a Special stationed at Gosport in Hampshire. In 1989 the business made a further move to Midhurst, in West Sussex, where I still operate the clock business. This move meant yet another transfer, this time, to the Sussex Police, based in Chichester.

I completed 25 years of service as a Special Constable while serving in the Sussex Police before retiring in 2000.

My mother's musical influence began to show through in later life, and at the age of 55 I decided to take up the piano with a passion. I have been very fortunate to have been helped, in my quest, by some unusually gifted tutors who have enabled me to become the resident organist in my Lodge. In 2007 I extended my musical experience by playing the Church organ (below). I became a volunteer organist in several of the churches in a local West Sussex Benefice, whilst receiving expert tuition and master classes from an outstanding former Cathedral Organist.

Postscript

My time in Barnardo's care may now be a distant memory but I feel thankful for the life that I have had and that I am still able to share it with my siblings. I believe that I have much to thank Barnardo's for in terms of the care provided for me and the preparation for my future life that they and their team gave me. Over the years there have been many people who have made a significant impact upon my life in a most positive way and I know that each and every one of them deserves my heartfelt thanks.

So here goes...

Deepest heartfelt thanks to **Mr James Dixon**, Headmaster of George Gascoigne School. "Taffy" was a diminutive man with an immense character and a huge and caring heart. He was a highly influential man to many of us and this was borne out of his fair-mindedness, compassion and understanding of those who had a 'rough' start to their lives.

Thanks Taffy

Many thanks to my mate of sixty years, **Brian**, for not only giving me my big break, at the Jeanetta Cochrane Theatre, but you also encouraged me and gave me a start in business in England's Lane in 1971.

Blimey matey if that wasn't enough you were also my Best Man. They broke the mould with you my very trusted friend.

My very special thanks to **Charlie Bide**, who I met at St Thomas's Hospital Engineers Department in 1969. A kind, mild-mannered gentleman who was very generous with his time and took me under his wing and gave me the strength and confidence to fly.

I miss you Charlie and think of you on a daily basis. God Bless you

Heartfelt thanks to "**Buggie**", **Mr Bugden**, who I met in Netheravon, in Wiltshire, in 1972. I was 26 years of age and he was 76 and I helped him with his awkward clock repairs and he helped and enabled me in a plethora of ways. A kind and selfless gentleman. I wouldn't be where I am today without you Buggie.

We hope you liked the flowers we left in Tenterden. God Bless You.

Finally let's end on a musical note - I really have "**No regrets**" in my life. I did it "**My Way**", once I had the opportunity, and now it just leaves me to conclude by saying "**Thanks for the Memories**"

Over and out!

William and Elizabeth would like to thank Vanessa of The White Space Design Co. for her high quality professionalism and assistance in the design and editing of our first book.

The Further Adventures
Of Peter The Tortoise